A GUIDE TO

ITALY

CULTURAL INSIGHTS AND TIPS TO MAXIMIZE YOUR TRIP

PATRICK TUNNO, PhD

ITALIAN
FIELDS
MEDIA

ITALIAN FIELDS MEDIA

Visit
www.italianfieldsmedia.com
www.patricktunnophd.com

Acknowledgments

I would like to acknowledge the following individuals whose expertise helped enrich the content in this book: Federico Antich, Stefano Baldassarri, Stefania Belli, Ida Castiglioni, Daniel Chiaravalli, Adelina Fiorucci, Gianni Marangio, Martina Mazzoleni, Paolo Pecorario, Michele Rumiz, Cassandra Santoro, Sonny Smith, and Franco Spaccialbelli.

Thanks to my editorial and production team, Tatiana Wilde and Stewart Williams.

Contents

The Beginning

Aunt Amelia's Cucina

My fascination with cultural differences can be traced back to my childhood. During a visit to my aunt's kitchen when I was twelve years old the tantalizing aroma of Italian cooking abruptly clashed with my expectations. This set me on a path to absorb everything I could about Italian culture. What I learned will help you find "la dolce vita" (the good life) on your visit to Italy.

During my first trip to my grandfather's small Italian village near L'Aquila, I smelled something delicious. From outside the white stuccoed house, I could hear the unmistakably lively sizzle of meat as it danced around a worn pan in my Aunt Amelia's kitchen. Hungry and curious, I wandered in from the patio, pushing the beaded Italian blinds aside, and looked directly across at my aunt. Although I was average-sized for my age, she was short and stocky; I was roughly the same height as this woman nearly sixty years older than me. Her face was obscured by thick, black-framed glasses and she seemed to always be wearing a V-shaped house-apron dress. Aunt Amelia spoke no English, and primarily the dialect of the Abruzzo region. I thought back to the phonetically written Italian phrases I had scribbled on a notepad before I came to Italy. Mustering up my courage, I attempted to ask if I could have a taste. She ignored me.

Aunt Amelia continued to flit around the kitchen, washing dishes and gathering scraps of food to set aside for her chickens. This time, I made a hand gesture of putting food into my mouth. She acknowledged me and slowly got a bowl, almost hesitating as she dished me out a small portion. I returned out to the patio and sat on a plastic chair to put the first steaming morsel in my mouth. Blah! This stuff smelled way better than it tasted. I was thinking

I'd just eat a few more bites, as to not offend her when she stuck her head out the door clutching the pan with the rest. "Oh, no," I thought. "Am I going to have to stomach more of this?" But before she got to me, Aunt Amelia turned the pan upside down and unceremoniously dumped the meat into a dish on the ground. Dick, the mangy-looking stray dog my aunt and uncle had adopted, lumbered over and happily slurped up his lunch. Then it hit me— I had just eaten dog food.

About twenty years later, I was once again eating on a patio in the Umbrian region of Italy. This time, I was around a dinner table at an *agriturismo,* a small farm that offers food and rooms for visitors. This one overlooked hilly terrain covered by green olive trees, overgrown grass, and bright red poppy flowers. Chickens and a few peacocks wandered the grounds below, while Todi, a medieval village that looks like it belongs in a snow globe, was perched on the steep hill above us. Three Penn State students and their host family smiled, laughed, and tried to communicate with each other. As an Italian professor, I served the dual role of cultural ambassador and translator. The students—three girls around nineteen—tried earnestly to talk to their new family but were completely ill-prepared. They had question after question, like: "How do you say I'm a vegetarian?" "Can you tell them the hot water doesn't work?" "Why is he peeling the skin off that pear?" "Do I have to drink all this wine?" "Is this water safe to drink?" "I can't eat anymore; do I have to?"

This time, I knew exactly what to say in Italian, how to behave, and every reason behind what was happening. Since then, I've dedicated myself to distilling this knowledge for others in the most simple and fun way possible. After my failed attempt to communicate with Aunt Amelia all those years earlier, I went through a metamorphosis. This book contains lessons learned, expert approaches, and practical information. It is the result of years of study, personal experiences in Italy, teaching multitudes of students, and personal interviews. It will give you a major advantage whether you are planning a vacation, business trip, or studying abroad in Italy. If I can go from Italian dog food taster to cultural maestro, then imagine what you can do.

An Italian Toolkit

Most travel guidebooks and forums provide you with lists of *what to do*. I give you the cultural knowledge you need and teach you *how to* approach the situations you will encounter so you can craft a meaningful, unforgettable, and authentic trip. This framework will take you much further than any guidebook could on its own. Whether you are traveling to Italy for work or pleasure, living there as an expat, or just love the country and want to delve a little deeper from the comfort of your armchair, the information in this book will provide you with an insider's perspective.

Instead of advice on visiting specific cities and tourist sites, you'll learn principles that blend cultural knowledge, context, and savvy travel practices. I also include some essential words and phrases that I've found to be especially helpful in navigating the culture. Having this in your toolkit will equip you with a baseline to artfully enter the landscape and experience the country on a deeper level. Learning how to approach travel with a *how-to* mindset may also benefit you beyond Italy. I view travel as more than visiting a place; it's connecting with the people that gives it meaning. My hope is that this book will provide you with the tools to open up aspects of Italy that may not be immediately accessible to the traveler, especially those traveling for short periods. In connecting with Italians and learning about the culture, your experiences can endure throughout your life and continue to inspire you.

A meaningful trip begins with experiencing and participating in the culture. Preeminent experts on culture Geert Hofstede, Gert Jan Hofstede, and Michael Minkov, in their book *Cultures and Organizations: Software of the Mind* stated, "Culture is learned, not innate. It derives from one's social environment rather than from one's genes."[1] Going with that analogy, the goal of this book will help you to function effectively in the cultural environment. While

---

[1] Geert Hofstede, Gert Jan Hofstede, Michael Minkov. *Cultures and organizations: Software of the mind.* (New York: McGraw-Hill, 2010), 6.

Italy can be extremely diverse in some respects, its customs are often similar across regions, so the great part is that once you learn the rules of the game, you can play anywhere.

Unlike a typical tourist guidebook, this book gives you the tools to understand, behave like, and connect with locals. You might ask, why does this matter? Well, think about the region where you live. Chances are, you can go into any store, restaurant, or business with confidence. You instinctively understand the expectations in day-to-day interactions. Simply put, locals blend in. They know how to identify a good restaurant, when the best times are to run errands, and how to avoid dicey situations. They are comfortable in their environment, don't stick out, are less likely to get taken advantage of, and typically make personal connections easily. Once you travel this way, you will improve your chances of gaining insights into the local culture, and realize that it is the most rewarding, meaningful way to experience Italy—or any country, for that matter.

What's more, tourists don't often have the best reputations. Why not represent your country with grace and good etiquette? My hope for you is that you leave Italy with something more than a collection of selfies and souvenirs. Whether you're wandering the cobblestone streets of a rural village or navigating a cosmopolitan urban landscape, my goal is to unlock the door so that you can experience meaningful and memorable encounters.

This book intentionally does not extensively cover history or subjects like "how to beat the line in the Vatican." There are countless travel guides and social media forums that address these topics. My approach marries culture and practical tips, while giving you space to unleash your curiosity. On the professional side, I've developed study abroad programs in Italy that promote cultural immersion, language learning, and personal growth. While from birth, when my traditional Neapolitan grandmother prayed to the saints that I'd be a boy (it worked), I was heavily influenced by my immigrant grandparents, and grew up Italian—or at least that's what I had thought. As a twelve-year-old kid, when I first visited our relatives in Italy, an affinity with the country slowly took root.

Years later, living with my uncle in Abruzzo and studying in Milan would transform my life. Through these formative experiences in Italy, I finally began to understand its essence. And, well, I just kept coming back.

Italy can be enchanting, with its hilltop vistas and golden horizons dotted with historic buildings and terracotta roofs, along with endless culinary, architectural, and artistic masterpieces. After all, it's the land that gave us gems including *cacio e pepe*, tiramisu, Botticelli, Stradivari, Michelangelo, and the Pantheon. Even in the routine, like observing smartly dressed morning commuters on bicycles and vespas, you will have your share of magical moments. As entertaining as the movie *Luca* was, Italy is no Disney film, and is certainly imperfect. When I was a young student, I idealized Italy. But, as with anywhere else, it has its good and bad qualities. I encountered sweet *nonna* (grandma) types, alongside refugees, the homeless, and chic, well-off locals. Some restaurateurs, shopkeepers, and locals treated me like a long-lost relative. Others viewed me suspiciously or even tried to take advantage of me, perhaps adding an unnecessary fee to my meal. Over the years, I've learned that understanding some basic cultural differences, words, and phrases can tip the scales.

As an informed traveler, you can expedite the cultural adjustment period, be a more confident traveler, save money, and help ensure your personal safety. With this knowledge, you can make smart use of your time. By engaging with the material in this book, my hope is that you'll prepare yourself for an enriching and transformational experience in *il bel paese* (the beautiful country), a very fitting nickname for this land.

I

Context that Sets the Stage

We seldom realize, for example, that our most private thoughts and emotions are not actually our own. For we think in terms of languages and images which we did not invent, but which were given to us by our society.
—ALAN W. WATTS

As you enter the Italian stage, you should know that some of the behaviors and norms in Italy are guided by unspoken rules and an underlying context. It's the result of thousands of years of history, recent events, social issues, and a unique culture. This chapter will provide you with a background on this context, insight into cultural norms, and tips that can help you become a smarter traveler. Included is a brief historical background, so you will have a sense of what you are seeing (and why), alongside some elements of the culture that are inescapable. Among the topics I've included are delightful cultural practices like *la passeggiata*, as well as subtexts such as mindset, that will impact your daily interactions with locals.

All Signs Point to Rome

If you don't know history, then you don't know anything. You are a leaf that doesn't know it is part of a tree.
—MICHAEL CRICHTON

One of Italy's most common street signs is Via Roma, which nearly always points in the direction of Rome; street names in Italy can also tell you about the broader or local history. If you are still looking for where street signs in Italy are located, look at the buildings on the corners of streets. Countless books, podcasts, and courses extensively explore the Italian peninsula's rich and long history, and while I won't get into that level of detail, I feel a basic understanding is essential for you to have a baseline for cultural awareness. If you are interested in an era or historical figure, I encourage you to engage in further reading.

As you visit Italy, you will see vestiges of its history all around you: large city gates that are hundreds of years old, the remains of Roman coliseums (yes, there was more than one), statues honoring artists, and avenues named for literary figures; ancient Greek theaters, churches from every era of Christianity or even rooted in paganism, as well as castles dotting the landscape. An indication of constant invasions is that many of Italy's small towns and cities sit on the top of hills, which made them defensible and now make for breathtaking views. You'll find monuments from the First and Second World Wars and streets that take their name from when Italy was liberated from German occupation (Via XXV Aprile, for instance). Garibaldi is another name of one of the most popular vias. Giuseppe Garibaldi is a figure who embodies Italy's unification in the nineteenth century. While the country has ancient origins, Italy was not unified until 1861, led by Garibaldi. The process was completed in 1870 when Rome and the territory of the Pope were added. This happened on September 20th, which is why you'll see streets named Via XX Settembre across the country.

For a historical timeline, let's start with the Etruscans, an ancient people who dominated the Italian peninsula until they were conquered by the Romans in the fifth century BCE. On a trip to Orvieto, a small Umbrian city perched on a rock cliff, I recall descending into an underground tunnel—part of a network of hundreds of caves carved out of the soft volcanic rock by the Etruscans. The Etruscans, under siege by the Romans, had dug underground cellars, shelters, storage areas, and wells, and lasted a few years in these structures, apparently capturing and eating pigeons, which you can still find on some Italian menus. Pre-dating the Romans, the Etruscan civilization was concentrated around Tuscany, which traces its name to Etruscan origins, and left behind many artifacts. They could be classified as the peninsula's first civilization; evidence of Etruscans appears around the ninth century BCE. Organized in tribes, they were rivals of the Greeks. During the Etruscan era, the Greeks colonized the area of southern Italy and Sicily known as Magna Graecia, and remnants of this civilization can be seen in the massive temples they left behind, such as at Paestum, about ninety minutes south of Naples.

The Romans, the most famous of Italy's civilizations, came to dominate Europe and nearby regions in the first century CE. The only period before modern Italy when the land was an autonomous united territory happened under Roman control. According to legend, Rome was founded by an orphan, Romulus, in 753 BCE. Along with his twin brother Remus, he was nursed by a she-wolf. As the story goes, Romulus later murdered his brother. This has been enshrined into folklore with an iconic sculpture, the Capitoline Wolf or Lupa Capitolina, depicting two boys suckling from the she-wolf. The statue's origins are unknown and may even go back to Etruscan times. Mussolini, Italy's infamous WWII dictator, had copies of the sculpture made and distributed worldwide. By 510 BCE, the Romans managed to expel the Etruscans from Rome, beginning an era of dominance. The Romans organized military operations and a system of government that contributed to centuries of influence, with famous emperors like Julius Caesar and Caesar Augustus. At its peak, the Roman Empire extended beyond modern Italy as far as England, North Africa, and the Middle East.

Romans were skilled engineers who created the aqueducts, coliseums, and street plans that are still visible in Italy today. Their cultural heritage gave the world the concept of a senate, gladiators, Roman numerals, and Latin, the foundation of many European languages. Roman emperor Marcus Aurelius's writings today impact the modern Stoicism philosophical movement. His personal journal, *Meditations*, is worth a look for anyone interested in self-reflection and philosophy. Ancient Rome had its own religion with numerous gods and goddesses. In the city of Rome, you will find very accessible Roman history to explore, as well as Pompeii, where in 79 CE, the eruption of Mount Vesuvius's volcano buried and preserved a Roman settlement.

In 330 CE, Constantine, who was emperor from 306 to 337 CE and converted to Christianity, moved the capital to Byzantium, which he renamed Constantinople and is known as Istanbul today. With essentially two capitals and increasingly fragmented, the Roman Empire became susceptible to invasions and started to fray. The rise of the pope in Rome as the head of the Catholic Church consolidated what was left of the remaining political capital. An alliance was formed with the Franks, a Germanic-speaking people who ruled some of the territories north of Italy, and Pope Leo III proclaimed Charlemagne as Holy Roman Emperor in 800 CE. Also, farther south, Muslims from North Africa invaded and occupied Sicily during this era. Today, you can see the Arab influence in Sicilian and Italian cuisine: they introduced citrus fruit, spinach, chickpeas, artichokes, eggplants, and even wheat, which made the production of pasta possible.

The papacy and Holy Roman Empire jockeyed for control. At the same time, cities across northern and central Italy seized the opportunity to form their own republics. These independent city states, such as Venice, Milan, Florence, Parma, and Verona, frequently warred with one another and conquered their neighbors. While in the southern half of the territory, Naples and Sicily were united into a kingdom by the Normans, descendants of Vikings who had settled in northern France. This kingdom had significant periods of prosperity as it became a center of commerce. Throughout this period, there were countless foreign invasions across the land. Spain and France were heavily involved and their influence on local dialects can still be observed. In the fifteenth century, the

Renaissance, fueled by wealthy families, took hold. Artistic treasures produced by giants of the Renaissance, including Michelangelo and Leonardo da Vinci, still define much of Italy's artistic heritage today. In the late eighteenth century, Napoleon Bonaparte entered the scene and conquered Italy, injecting French concepts of equality and patriotism. When he combined the disparate territories into a Kingdom of Italy, the people he ruled began to envision the possibility of an Italian nation. Eventually, Napoleon fell, and other foreign powers split Italy into several states. However, the dream of a nation endured, with a movement—the Risorgimento—born to unite Italy through political and military actions. This culminated with Giuseppe Garibaldi famously unifying the country in 1861. Victor Emmanuel was proclaimed king of Italy, and a parliament was formed. However, Italy remained regionally distinct, and the Vatican became its own state, as it remains today.

In the twentieth century, Italy entered a phase of colonial ambitions, attempting to conquer territories in the region as well as further afield, in countries such as Eritrea, which became a colony. After the First World War, Italy annexed additional territory in Europe, including Trieste and Trentino. In the following years, Benito Mussolini, self-proclaimed *"Il Duce"* (the Leader), formed the nationalistic Fascist Party. With aspirations of returning to the glory of ancient Rome, he modernized the military and country, reigniting colonial ambitions. In 1940, Italy allied with Nazi Germany but experienced extensive defeats in its war efforts. In 1943, Mussolini was forced out of power and fled to establish a government in Salò, a town in the region of Lombardy, and Italy declared war on Germany. Northern Italy was liberated in 1945 by Allied forces and partisans, and Mussolini was executed.

After the war, Italy abolished the monarchy, jettisoned its colonies, and became a republic, with the Prime Minister serving as its head. In the years that followed, Italy cycled through numerous governments and challenges. While Italy enjoyed economic success in the post-war period, antiquated bureaucracy, public corruption, the specter of a violent communist takeover by the Red Brigades, and organized crime has made the landscape challenging. Italy joined the EU as a member state in 1958 and the European Monetary Union in 1999, establishing the euro as its currency. Italian politics today remain messy, and the country has votes of no confidence and a new government every few years.

Mindset

THE REGIONAL ITALIAN MINDSET

Geography, traditions, and history play a role in the presence of unique regional mindsets. "Canto degli Italiani" is the official anthem of the Italian Republic. It calls for Italians from the Alps to Sicily to unite under one flag, reminding us that for centuries Italians were divided. Before its unification in 1861, Italy comprised many different nation-states, with some of them speaking different languages. One of the most noticeable differences remains between the north and south. When southern Italy voted to join the new nation of Italy, it believed it would have autonomy, but Italy's center of power was skewed to the north. Huge taxes were levied on the south, which was also subjected to military conscription, and policies favored the industrial northern part of the country. There were attempts to rebel in Naples and Sicily, but they were quickly quashed, and even summary executions took place.

In an effort to regain some control, public corruption emerged, and power balances are still a huge issue. In 2020, unemployment in the north was 5.8 percent, while in the south it was 15.9 percent. In recent years, the number of Italians living in poverty has been approximately 5 to 6 percent in the north, and nearly 20 percent in the south. If you meet an Italian abroad and ask where they are from, they might offer the city or region before saying "I'm Italian." While in some areas of the US the streets are lined with flags or patriotic decorations, this is uncommon in Italy. While living in Milan, I was often told by my Milanese friends that they are more *aperti* (open) and *calorosi* (warm) in the southern half of the country. The Catholic Church and traditional, family values seem to have a stronger hold in the south, whereas in the northern regions, it's said that Italians are more career-focused and reliant on the role of community. Their personalities are sometimes characterized as *freddi* (cold) by their southern neighbors. While from an economic standpoint, the south may have lower standards of living, as a people, they tend to be happy. Much of the southern population benefits from strong family ties, warm weather, and coastal living, which may impact their outlook.

Italy groups the following regions together:

- *Northwest*: Piedmont, Valle d'Aosta (Vallée d'Aoste), Liguria, Lombardy
- *Northeast*: Trentino Alto Adige (Südtirol), Veneto, Friuli-Venezia Giulia, Emilia-Romagna
- *Central*: Tuscany, Umbria, Marche, Lazio
- *Southern*: Abruzzo, Molise, Campania, Puglia, Basilicata, Calabria, Sicily, Sardinia

THE CONCEPT OF TIME

In America, one must be something, but in Italy one can simply be.
—PIETROS MANEOS

Being Italian can be more about living in the moment than a laser focus on a certain objective. Italians tend to have a polychronic orientation, meaning they may be easily distracted by competing priorities. During a few of my interviews for this book, I saw this firsthand as some of the Italians I interviewed were interrupted by others, took phone calls, or even tended to the stove. The cultural tendency is to use time to accomplish what is needed rather than focus on one specific goal. Personal time and relationships often are the priority. While this is true throughout Italy, northern Italy conforms more to its action-oriented European neighbors. At the same time, the further south you go time becomes more flexible. Another way to look at this is having a sense of being versus doing. Italians prioritize time to speak with family and friends. Much more than Americans, Italians will frequently spend time around the dinner table during meals when in the company of family and friends.

THE LEGACY OF THE CATHOLIC CHURCH

Over the years, the number of Italians who attend church has declined. Only about 25 percent of Italians attend mass at least once a week, while roughly the same amount never step inside. There is greater participation in southern Italy and with older populations. Despite this shift, the Catholic Church still fundamentally impacts the Italian mindset. The artistic heritage that came from the Church is ubiquitous in Italy, with the Catholic values it represents still informing how Italians view the world. Turn the TV on to Rai Italia, Italian's public national television network on Sunday, when you will find it broadcasting Catholic mass.

And, of course, churches are everywhere, their bell towers dominating the landscape of every village, city, and town. Their daily ringing is a reminder of the Church's presence and is ingrained into the rhythm of life and Italian subconscious. As the head of the Catholic Church, the Pope is a massive figure and another frequent sight on national TV. Beyond this, religion is woven into the cultural fabric of Italy, with most major festivals and holidays having religious origins. One could argue that the paternalistic orientation that many Italians share could be partially traced back to the Church. This outlook means that those with greater resources should care for those who don't have as much. Perhaps the Italian sense of chivalry, with how men treat women, holding doors and paying the check at a restaurant, for example, may even be vestiges of its enduring influence.

COLLECTIVE RITUALS

Chi mangia da solo si strozza is an Italian proverb that means "he who eats alone suffocates." Italians are exceptionally social and gravitate toward people and the collective. I chatted about the idea of a collective mindset with Ida Castiglioni, a professor of the sociology of cultural processes at the University of Milano-Bicocca. She talked about the collective ritual of an August beach vacation. Ida pointed out that if you go to the beaches in August, you will notice that the umbrellas seem positioned remarkably close to each other and that there is almost a cocktail party-like atmosphere. Italians will go to the beach in groups, but they'll also socialize with the people around them who they don't know. While Italians are strongly pulled to collective rituals, traditions, and activities, they want to be valued as individuals. At the beach, this shows up when they display modern-day status symbols such as watches, swim outfits, and tattoos nowadays.

Another example of collective Italian behavior is in their lunch ritual. While American workers may eat at their desks at just about any time, Italians go out at a set time, and nearly everyone does this. Restaurants are filled with workers from 1:30-3 pm every day; it's a social activity and part of their cultural identity. This sense of togetherness is the basis of Italian society. At the same time, individuality is expressed through clothing, family identity, and brands. Ida quipped that she recently bought a cutting board and noticed that even it had a brand, indicating that the Italian family who made it wanted to leave its mark.

FAMILIES AND CLOSE COMMUNITIES

The role of the family is an essential part of how Italians view the world. The family is the nucleus of life for many Italians, and they will likely be happy to talk about theirs. In fact, this can be a great topic to connect with locals as you share information about your own. You may find the family dynamics unexpected, so some context is important. Nearly half of 25-34-year-old Italians live at home with their parents. Extending this to eighteen years of age, two thirds of Italians live in their family homes, which may include multiple generations under the same roof. This phenomenon is even more pronounced for men, with 70 percent of them in this age group living with their parents. Typically, those who have the means to leave their parents' homes do so after age thirty. Economics is one of the reasons that young Italians stay at home; it can be challenging to find a good-paying job, and living expenses are high. It's not very common for young Italians to have jobs, as you might expect in some countries where the summer job is considered a rite of passage. In addition, youth unemployment remains very high. Some young Italians are not engaged in economically productive activities, with nearly 22 percent of 18-29-year-olds neither studying nor working.

However, perhaps an even more significant reason Italians live at home is their strong ties to family, hometown, and traditions, which as a visitor you will likely observe. They desire to stay where they grew up, surrounded by lifelong friends. They find comfort in knowing their family can care for them and their children, and that they can care for their own parents and relatives. Italians may be willing to accept the tradeoff of lower economic conditions for what they perceive as a higher quality of life. Because of this focus on intimate, lifelong connections, Italians tend to be very tight knit and seem to have a rapport with everyone in town. While you may make friends in smaller towns where outsiders are less common, it can be nearly impossible to break into their inner circle.

Social Issues

IMMIGRATION

Some visitors are surprised that many residents in Italy are not stereotypically Italian. I feel it's important to shed some light on those you will encounter for both context and empathy. Italy historically was a country of emigrants, and the phenomenon of being a destination for immigrants, particularly those not of European origins, is relatively new. The non-citizen population in Italy is approximately five million, which is significant in a country that has a population of just under sixty million people. In the last decade, more than one million individuals acquired Italian citizenship. In terms of numbers, the following nationalities rank the highest: Albanians, Moroccans, Romanians, Brazilians, Indians, Argentines, Peruvians, Tunisians, French, and Macedonians. Romanians have become the largest concentration of non-Italians to migrate to Italy, which makes sense as Romania is an EU member and its language is similar.

Between 2011 and 2021, there were 516,000 asylum claims granted to citizens from Pakistan, Nigeria, Egypt, Mali, and the Ivory Coast, among others. As of 2021, 236,000 refugees from Ukraine were present in Italy, as a consequence of the Russian conflict. These refugees have headed primarily to Milan, Rome, Naples, and Bologna. Yet, these are not the only ethnic groups you will notice.

I first became attuned to a Chinese presence in Italy while living in Milan more than twenty years ago. I was surprised to eat at a Chinese pizzeria, and one of the regular lunch spots for students in my MBA program at SDA Bocconi University was a budget-friendly, Chinese-Italian restaurant. During a meal with a Japanese classmate, it felt odd to see a Chinese waiter and my classmate communicate in imperfect Italian, as Masaki ordered *riso cantonese* (a Cantonese rice dish). Looking back, it makes sense as the Japanese and Chinese have different origins. In my travels back to Italy, I've discovered immigrant-run eateries that produce nearly indistinguishable Italian food. Having a culture that is more distant from Italy than other nations, such as Romania and Albania, the Chinese populations tend to cluster geographically. Major areas include Rome and Prato in Tuscany. Currently, there are more than 300,000 Chinese residents, most of whom immigrated as families. The Chinese also remain distant in another way: even most of those born in Italy to Chinese parents still tend to think in their Chinese language rather than Italian. Other immigrant populations, such as Egyptians, do not immigrate as families and have an uneven gender balance in Italy. Twice as many men from Egypt immigrate than women. This likely indicates that their migration is driven by labor. Most Egyptians are concentrated in Rome and Milan.

Ida Castiglioni mentioned that the students studying abroad in Italy are struck by the people of color serving as "riders" or *fattorini* (delivery workers) transporting food by bicycle in cities for companies like Uber Eats. Looking into this further, there are numerous articles about how illegal immigrants are delivering food. It was reported in Milan's *Corriere della Sera* that these migrants are being exploited. Some accounts say they are recruited as workers and pressured to work for low pay and under challenging conditions. Because they don't have legal status in Italy, others let them assume their identities to create an employment account in exchange for a cut of the worker's earnings.

EQUITY

Even though this topic may be controversial, I felt it was important to include it, especially for longer term visitors or students studying in Italy. The American concept of equity is viewed differently across Europe and Italy. Fairness may be a universal principle, but its interpretation can be cultural. I interviewed numerous Italians working in higher education who mentioned that some Europeans feel US students can have what they would consider a sanctimonious view of the concept of equity. Some Italians have characterized these student perspectives as outrage at what are perceived as injustices. Let me be clear, I'm not expressing my own opinion here or advocating a personal agenda, but I feel it's important to be careful when imposing something that may be accepted in your circles onto another culture. In addition, don't be shocked if you or others from your culture perceive injustices in the equity space.

One issue pointed out was that, in Italy, graduates in engineering earn little more than €1,200 per month net for the first few years. This is barely enough to cover rent in cities like Rome and Milan. The Italians I spoke with said that some Americans try to tell them this is not right and that they should fight the system. Remember, Italians know the system better than you, so it's better to listen and try to understand rather than attempt to solve their problems or point out injustices. Doing this will allow you to avoid making a *brutta figura* (poor impression, see Chapter III) and enable you to focus more on having a positive experience.

Cultural Practices and Unspoken Rules

PASSEGGIATA

In the late afternoon and after dinner, from small towns to large cities, the notion of la *passeggiata* is cemented as an Italian cultural practice. After the lunch hour, stores gradually come back to life. Italians freshen up, get dressed in stylish clothes, and stroll the main *corso* (avenue), piazzas, or important streets in the historic center. During weekdays, by the late afternoon, workers who have finished the day might take to the streets for pre-dinner *aperitivo*. You may see couples enjoying one another's company, the young flirting, families socializing, and grandparents that treat their grandchildren to a gelato. Regardless, the idea is to be seen and connect with others. Large and visible shop windows, called *vetrine*, boast artfully displayed products that passersby admire. Locals may stop for a coffee or drink while people-watching. In smaller cities, it feels like one big cocktail party. Friends and acquaintances smile and say hello, often greeting each other with kisses on either side of the cheek. As you approach the piazza of the main street, you'll hear spirited chatter before you even catch a glimpse of crowds of people enjoying each other's company. By dinner, the activity simmers down, with some people returning to cap off the evening with a walk and gelato or to experience a drink and socialize. You may notice the young and old lingering in the piazzas into the late evening, sipping a beverage or glass of wine among friends. As a visitor, participation in a *passeggiata* is a rite of passage. Don't miss this opportunity to get dressed up and enjoy experiencing local life.

ITALIAN SCHOOL

If you pay attention to the local rhythms, you'll notice that Italian children return home around the lunch hour each day. Through high school, Italy's educational institutions typically run from around 8 am until 1 pm. Students often return home by the lunch hour, and it isn't uncommon for lunch to be prepared by the grandparents if the parents work. When parents work nearby, they may join the family lunch, though this practice is becoming less frequent. In high school and the grades below, students have classes on both weekdays and Saturdays. In larger cities, there are some exceptions where schools offer a *settimana corta* (short week). Saturdays are off if the hours can be made up during the week. Schools are closed from June to September, and students go to high school until they are nineteen years old. Secondary schools are specialized in disciplines such as the arts, liberal arts, science, and technical fields.

At universities, bachelors programs take three years to complete, and a master's degree is earned in two additional years, while doctoral programs require further study. Public universities are much different in terms of facilities and student services than what you might find in the US. They may appear neglected, and the notion of student services and support is virtually nonexistent. Professors typically show up and lecture but don't provide much homework or seem to care whether students attend class. Final grades are often determined by a single exam at the end of the semester. University students may live at home or in apartments near the school, and there is usually a very modest amount of university housing. The American concepts of sports teams, mascots, school spirit, and rivalries are not part of the climate. Most campuses are embedded into the city, so large, sprawling, or isolated campuses are uncommon. Italian students primarily study at home or in the library. Doing work in a coffee shop or café with notes sprawled out and a laptop open is a nonexistent practice in Italy.

WAITING IN LINES

The Italian version of waiting in lines can be disorganized and doesn't follow rules. I talked with Gianni Marangio, who has worked for Temple University's Rome campus for decades. He shared an anecdote where he took some American students on an excursion to a small village in Umbria. When they prepared a buffet of food for the students, he seemed astonished that three orderly lines seemed to magically appear without any instruction to do so. Comparing this to Italian behavior, the outcome would be a jumbled mass of people buzzing around the table, with someone shouting to form a line and no one listening. When in line in Italy, the clerk often blurts out, *"Chi è il prossimo?"* (Who's next in line?). Italians seem to instinctively know who is in front of them, simply asking *"Chi è l'ultimo?"* A caveat to this is the *furbo* (sneaky) person who is way back in the queue and declares to the person at the front of the line, "I just have to ask a quick question." Without fail, this quick question ends up being some absurdly complicated request. Occasionally, the other customers get agitated and will challenge the person disrespecting the social order. They might say, "I was here first," or come to the rescue of whomever was before the offender. Don't be shocked if someone cuts right in front of you. You can politely remind them that you were there first.

NEGOTIATING

In Italy, rules may be negotiable if you are culturally attuned. For example, during a several-month work assignment, I lived across the Italian border in Switzerland. I bought a watch as a gift in

Como, Italy. If I could get it stamped at the border, I could return to the shop for a large tax refund. I asked the Italian border officials, who directed me to the Swiss border officer on the other side of the street. The Swiss officer said he couldn't help, but he glanced at the booth on the Italian side and said, "They'll do it, go ahead and try again." So somewhat comically, I walked only a few steps and recrossed the border. I pleaded my case to the Italian officials, saying the Swiss border control sent me back. Then I said something like, *"Ma dai non si può fare qualcosa? Vi prego."* (Come on, can't you do something? I'm begging you.). I explained why the gift was so meaningful with maybe just a touch of an emotional sob story. Then, poof, they opened a drawer, pulled out a stamp, and officially marked my receipt. In this case, I think using the Italian language made a difference. While this is one of my favorite episodes illustrating this tactic, this behavior has happened to me repeatedly. On another occasion, I had been planning a dinner with a large group in Tivoli. The restaurant had a fascinating feature. The owners discovered a hidden wall dating back to Roman times, complete with artifacts that diners could check out. Unfortunately, I was informed they were no longer taking groups. When I lamented to the front desk worker at my hotel in Rome, he called and pleaded, saying how much it would mean to us. Miraculously, they booked us on the spot.

PERSONAL SPACE

Compared to Anglo-Saxon cultures, Italians have a different notion of personal space and can be tactile. "Italians are touchy people and extremely friendly," one of my Italian friends said. Even during Covid-19, the idea of social distancing was three feet as opposed to six in many other countries. They will likely be closer to you in line or on public transportation, and friends may grab each other's arms, hold hands, and touch more than you may expect.

SOCIAL NETWORKS

I've known Stefania Belli, CEO & Director at The Language Center in Todi, for more than a decade. She added some context for me on the function of social networks in Italy when she brought up the ancient origins of many rules and laws. In fact, there is an Italian expression, *Fatta la legge, trovato l'inganno*, which can be translated to "There's a loophole in every law." Sometimes, the laws and rules aren't clear, and not everyone follows them. Because of this, it can feel like nothing works. Instead, Italians have found ways to improvise, which Stefania thinks is one of the Italians' greatest strengths. She said you might call a government office with a problem, only to find no one answers, but by using your social network, you find out who can help you out of a situation. This is something Italians seem to always figure out.

As a visitor, rather than getting frustrated, improvise. Who do you know? Could a hotel worker, your landlord, a local guide, or a friend you made at the bar down the street help? Use your network to be resourceful when facing a challenge. Chances are, they know someone who can help. I recall once needing to take a student for a medical check in Naples in the early morning hours. When we arrived at the hospital, the gates were locked. At a complete loss for what to do, I asked two guys who appeared to be coming back from a night out. They told me to hold on and called a phone number. "Okay, the doctor will come to you." A few minutes later, an ambulance showed up and evaluated the student on the spot. I find that local knowledge is always the best in a country that revolves around relationships to problem solve.

II

Food and Drink

Mangiare per vivere non vivere per mangiare.
(Eat to live, don't live to eat.)
—ITALIAN PROVERB

Food is the epitome of cultural identity. The ingredients, history, and traditions that surround it tell us a story. If you want to know a culture, you must know the food. Italian cuisine is iconic, romanticized, and according to *U.S. News & World Report* in 2021, the best in the world. Eating in Italy is also unavoidable. After your arrival, addressing your appetite will likely be a top priority once you get settled. Regardless of your itinerary, you'll refuel multiple times a day, or maybe dozens if you share my insatiable love for fresh gelato and bold espresso. Glance at any cookbook, watch an Italian cook in their kitchen, or eat enough meals throughout the country and you will notice that recipes are simple and rely on a few, fresh, seasonal ingredients. Cuisine hinges on what is available locally, which explains the regional differences in Italian gastronomy (what we can call the art of good cooking and eating). For example, olive oil is synonymous with Italian cooking. But it is used more in southern Italian cooking where olives grow well and are plentiful. Butter and milk, on the other hand, have been staples in the northern regions, which have abundant cattle. This dairy belt primarily spans four regions, across Piedmont to Veneto and from Lombardy down to Emilia-Romagna.

There are also fascinating geographic peculiarities. As you

approach the border with Austria, the regional food of Alto Adige begins to mirror what you might expect to find in Germanic cultures, such as strudel filled with apples, raisins, and cinnamon. In fact, most of Alto Adige's residents speak German. From the interior of the island region of Sardinia a crispy flatbread called *pane carasau* has historical origins as a convenient, long-lasting staple to eat during excursions to move livestock. My own grandfather used to tell me how he would spend all day as a boy tending sheep in the mountains above his *Abruzzese* village with not much more than a hunk of dry bread. Across the country, Italians celebrate both their roots and locally available fruits and vegetables, choosing fresh produce when it's in season.

To give some perspective on regional differences in Italian food, consider the relatively homogenized cuisine of the United States. Despite the standard American diet, many areas have their specialties, such as Maine lobsters, gumbo in New Orleans, southern barbeque, or Tex-Mex cuisine. Italy's twenty regions are divided into approximately one hundred provinces and comprised of nearly eight thousand municipalities. Each has diverse cultural traditions that have been steeped in thousands of years of history. Italy is a country of stark geographic divisions, including massive mountain ranges and hills, rivers that slice the country into sections, and two regions that are entire islands. Until its unification in 1861, it was a series of different nation-states, all with distinct local dialects. This regionalism played a huge part in the birth of Italian food and each region, province, and small town has its own unique specialties. In landlocked parts of the Tuscan interior, you won't likely find fish on the menu, though you might see wild boar with pappardelle pasta. In Italy's southern regions, which jut into the sea, entrees like squid, shellfish, and prawns could be center stage.

If you'd like to learn more about Italian cuisine, I suggest consulting *il Cucchiaio d'Argento* (The Silver Spoon). Traditionally a wedding gift for Italian brides, it is like your very own master class on Italian food that compiles more than 2,000 recipes from various towns and regions. Italians are immensely proud of their regional foods. Learn to be curious. Think of dining as a food adventure. Don't always seek familiar things like spaghetti with tomato sauce or pizza. Ask questions at restaurants or markets. Italians know their local traditions, customs, and cuisine. Waitstaff, vendors, and market workers have highly specialized knowledge. They can tell you about local dishes and make recommendations.

Slow Food

In 1986, when fast food behemoth McDonald's opened its doors in Rome's iconic Piazza di Spagna, protests erupted. Locals wanted to preserve the hundreds of years of history and traditions that embody the food landscape cutting across Italy, and the Slow Food movement took root. Today, the movement aims to sustain rural communities and offers authentic food experiences. It's a useful lens to understand how Italians view food. If you understand it, you'll get a higher quality product at a better price. And as a bonus, you'll learn something that connects you to the culture.

"People underestimate Italy's diversity in terms of local cultures and local gastronomy. Every valley, subregion, and province is divided into cultural and gastronomic identities with their own specificity. A lifetime wouldn't be enough to know them all," says Michele Ruiz, Slow Food Travel director. According to Michele, "When we talk Slow Food wherever we are, regardless of tourism, we always encourage people to enter the matrix and go beyond the recipes." He says that if you understand the ingredients from a 360 degree perspective, you'll begin to understand gastronomy. The interaction between people and the environment produces a unique quality of products. In doing so, you'll get to know the farmers, artisans, and heritage.

As you navigate this phenomenal food scene, I recommend that you gravitate toward local products and regional dishes from the areas you visit. This will help ensure you experience the highest quality products while learning about the culture. Michele mentioned that going off the beaten path can connect you to the most authentic identities. He added, "Often tourism consumes the assets expected to provide. In the Amalfi coast, finding the real food producers or stories gets harder and harder because everybody is now on tourism. If you go to Venice, it's basically an empty city. It's like Disneyland. It isn't alive with locals." But if you travel around Venice's lagoon, you find food gardens, wine, and artichoke productions. There are farms in the middle of the small islands. You still find exotic trees that have nothing to do with Italy that grew from seeds Venetian merchants brought and planted in the middle of the lagoons. With the Slow Food movement, there's a fantastic richness where you can encounter communities and their identities. Michele explained, "You can lose quality and restore it over time, but if you lose identity, there's no way to restore it. Food identities belong to communities, not to individuals. It needs to be a shared definition of identity, and this is exactly what we try to preserve." The Slow Food movement "safeguards these local identities of food that, in a way, have all the elements that can lead to sustainable development for these communities."

Made in Italy

FOOD EXCELLENCE

Italian food has long been recognized for its quality, partly due to the traditional and labor-intensive efforts undertaken to produce agricultural products. And, of course, from prosciutto to Parmigiano, there have been countless attempts to imitate them or even appropriate their names. To distinguish the authentic from the inferior, if not counterfeit, products, the European Union established a framework of protected designation of origin products. Protected Designation of Origin (PDO) or Denominazione di Origine Protetta (DOP) in Italian, is the highest certification of foods or condiments (such as olive oils) linked to a territory. The raw materials must be from, and the entire production process must occur in, that designated region. Protected Geographical Indication (PGI), or Indicazione Geografica Protetta (IGP) in Italian, is the following classification level. Though less rigorous, it still guarantees an exceptional product, with significant production, processing, or preparation occurring in the region.

This matters because it means that historical know-how is behind it. It means that when you buy a piece of PDO Parmigiano Reggiano cheese, you know it was made in a central region of Italy, spanning the Apennine ridge to the Po River. Parmigiano is strictly regulated, using only fresh milk from this area. The cows can only be milked twice daily and fed a special diet linked to the region. Historically, monks developed the cheese-making method centuries ago to save excess milk. As the milk simmered during cooking, they stirred it with a thorny branch, resulting in the cheese's appealing texture. Today, it's made in copper vats and mixed with a unique spiky tool called a *spina*. After it's placed on forms, it will be aged at least twelve months. The result is a distinct, sharp, and complex taste, with a granular sensation as you bite into it. Many consumers never realize that Parmigiano is an entirely different product than the non-Italian parmesan cheeses you find abroad. The Parmigiano Reggiano Consortium's website (www.parmigianoreggiano.com) is a terrific resource if you want to learn more.

Conversely, if you see products in your home country that read "imported from Italy" or "produced in Italy," the origins are actually a mystery. This is often the case with olive oil from Greek, Spanish, or Moroccan olives. With this general designation, there's no indication that the raw materials came from Italy. You only know that it was finished there or passed through Italy before it was imported elsewhere. Given the country's obsession with quality food, a product's Italian roots make a big difference.

WINE MAKES YOU SING

Growing up, whether in the US or in Italy, when my family would get together, there was always wine. While it was never overconsumed, at the end of a meal, as we sat around the table, we'd occasionally break out into this Italian folk song. It begins with *L'Acqua Fa Male il Vino Fa Cantare* (Water is Unhealthy but Wine Makes You Sing) and ends with *Bevilo tutto* (Drink it all). Although for some it may be a drinking song, which is generally impolite in Italy, it demonstrates how wine is paired with food and family as it is firmly embedded into the culture. Wine is where history, geography, science, and culture converge into a simple beverage. More than half of the Italian population regularly drinks wine, with many Italians consuming it daily. While it's been a longstanding staple, over the years, wine has become more associated with status. Those who can discuss the story behind a vintage and how it connects to the territory are seen as interesting, cultured individuals. You don't need to be an expert to enjoy it, but being curious can take you deeper into the culture. If you're not an oenophile (wine connoisseur), I will cover a few of the basics.

If you're not an expert and want to ensure you're getting a top-quality wine, you should be aware of the classification system. Wine is regulated, and there are various levels that distinguish it, which you will see right on the labels. *Denominazione di Origine Controllata e Garantita* (DOCG) is the strictest designation for Italian wines with a "guarantee" that they are the highest quality. While slightly less regulated, *Denominazione di Origine Controllata* (DOC) is a very highly controlled wine with specific rules on the origin of the grapes and the production methods. While not as rigid, *Indicazione Geografica Tipica* (IGT) is still representative of a wine typical of the geographical region. Of course, there are many outstanding wines in Italy that do not have any designation, but knowing this system can give you some confidence of the product's quality. It's easy to do a deep dive into the hundreds of varieties of wine so I'll highlight just a few. From the northern part of the country come favorites such as Pinot Grigio, Nebbiolo, sparkling Prosecco, and Sauvignon Blanc. In central Italy, you will find Chianti and reds from Montefalco, along with Merlot, Sangiovese, Montepulciano, and Cabernet Sauvignon. As you move further south, there are even wines that arise from volcanic soil, such as Taurasi, Fiano, and Greco, or from the Puglia region robust reds including Primitivo, while Sicily produces wine made from Nero d'Avola. Regardless of the variety, as with the cuisine from any region you visit, I'll suggest you sample the local varieties. At restaurants, you may hear the term *vino della casa* (house wine). In Italy, this is typically a local variety, decent quality, and affordable, that is served in a small carafe.

Eating Out

A CASA (AT HOME)

La cucina piccola fa la casa grande. This Italian proverb translates to "a small kitchen makes the house big." I know a house is not a restaurant. But, before we delve into the dining scene, as part of your cultural knowledge, you should know that Italians don't regularly eat many meals outside of their homes. The exception is when they cannot get home during the work week. Even picking up take-out, fast food, or prepared meals is infrequent. Instead, sitting around the table for dinner and lunch when possible is customary. Even if dinner, traditionally a much lighter meal than lunch, is some modest sliced meats, salad, cheese, and fruit, Italians gather together at roughly the same time. Having snack foods or breakfast for dinner isn't part of the culture. Another practice you won't see is eating meals and snacks on a sofa while watching television. Unless you are invited to someone's house, of course, you won't have the chance to eat *a casa*, but you can always recreate this by going to a market yourself and embracing an at-home meal in the Italian style.

QUICK AND CONVENIENT

Italians know how to start the day, sipping a cappuccino or espresso in the local coffee bar while savoring a jam or chocolate-filled croissant, known as *brioche* (a French term) in the north or *cornetto* in the rest of Italy. As a visitor doing a lot of exploring, you'll probably quickly burn through this morning sugar rush and will likely find yourself ready for lunch by 11:00 am. If you have real fortitude, you might power through until noon. But you'll quickly discover that Italian restaurants appear like a mirage, mysteriously open for business around 1:30 pm (a bit earlier in the north). By 4:00 pm, the last patron has polished off an espresso and already sauntered home for a nap. The doors quietly shut, not reopening until at least 7:30 pm. For some, it would seem they are doomed to wander the cobblestone streets in a state of constant hunger. To complicate matters, for those budget-minded, dining at a *ristorante* (restaurant) is one of the fastest ways to burn through cash. A moderately priced meal at a restaurant could start around €35 per person. Later, we'll get into how an Italian restaurant dining experience differs from what you may be used to. We'll also cover the choreographed movements common to all table service eateries. But first, because not all meals may be at formal restaurants, let's go over some ways to save a few euros.

Pizza and panini are good solutions for many travelers to avoid higher-priced food. During my graduate studies in Italy, I often refueled at lunchtime with a sandwich purchased at a coffee bar or a slice of pizza from the *panificio* (bakery) near my school. Italian prosciutto, cheese, bread, and pizza are indeed world-renowned. But, after a few days, you'll likely conclude there can be too much of a good thing. In school, I recall joking with a classmate from Greece that we should just cut to the chase by buying a bag of flour and eating it with a spoon. He gave me a look of sympathetic desperation. My advice is to find a *tavola calda*!

Tavola Calda and Rosticceria

This is one of my favorite ways to eat in Italy. Particularly in northern and central regions, it is the equivalent of a cafeteria or the prepared foods counter in a supermarket. You can get a well-balanced, nutritious meal for about €15 without being charged a *coperto* (a service charge to cover the bread and the privilege of sitting down). There's a great deal of variation in quality and offerings in these eateries, and as with many Italian small businesses, they are typically mom-and-pop shops. The counter will display an array of prepared pastas, rice salads, vegetables, meats, etc. The visual aspect is a bonus for folks with limited language skills. Simply wander in and point to what you want. You'll typically be charged by the weight or portion size. Another convenience is they may open as early as 10-11 am and remain open until 8-9 pm.

While accompanying a group to Rome's Vatican Museum, during a lunch break, I looked around at the cluster of tourist-catering restaurants across the street and intentionally went in the opposite direction. A few blocks later, the tourists disappeared, and I spotted *Rosticceria De Santis*. Inside, genuine people were smiling behind a humble counter displaying reasonably priced food to please the most discerning Italian grandmother. Wandering away from the tourist hotspots and just looking in the windows can pay off. It's also an adventurous way to immerse yourself in the food scene. You'll find seating at a *tavola calda* or *rosticceria*, but not table service with a waitstaff. Because you pay at the counter before eating, you can enjoy a fast lunch without waiting on service or the bill. They will pack up food to go, which can be handy if you'd prefer to dine on takeaway where you're staying.

The Pizzeria

Although it's another way to incorporate carbs into your life, you can eat cheaply at a pizzeria. Pizzas arrive hot, fresh, and typically much thinner than American-style pie, though some shops specialize in thick slices. Pizzas are not precut, and a whole one is intended to be an individual serving. Italians usually eat them with a knife and fork like a steak. Toppings could be pretty different from what you might expect. You should note that in Italy, *peperoni* (spelled with one less "p") refers to peppers; to order the equivalent of American pepperoni, ask for *pizza alla diavola*. This means pizza with spicy pepperoni (cured meat). You will notice that most Italians prefer beer, water, or a soft drink with pizza rather than wine. Thin-style Italian pizza is phenomenal out of the oven but gets soggy quickly. It's uncommon for Italians to take their leftovers to go, and with pizza, this is especially the case. The name pizzeria can be just the tip of the iceberg, as salads and other entrees are often available. For example, Como has an unassuming shop named Bar Pizzeria da Quinto. It looks like a hole in the wall (often, the best restaurants do) but on my visits there, I found patrons clamoring at the counter, ordering thick pizza slices and an array of hot prepared foods. Just outside the door, locals dressed in casual elegance, along with men in sports jackets and jeans, hung out sipping aperitifs as they chatted with friends and watched the people pass by. I recall heading there one evening after my flight landed in Italy. I walked out with pizza, fried fish, and assorted vegetables to enjoy as I recharged and unpacked in my apartment. Pizzerias typically follow the standard operating hours as a restaurant, opening from lunch around 1:30 pm until 3:30 pm and opening again for dinner at 7:30 or 8:00 pm.

The Aperitivo

An *aperitivo* is the notion of having a drink before a meal to whet your appetite. In Italy, this traditionally involves a beverage with low alcohol content and is accompanied by snacks. The students at my graduate school and I would view an *aperitivo* as an opportunity for all-you-can-eat hors d'oeuvres. All that's required is to purchase a drink such as a beer, wine, spritz, or even something nonalcoholic. *Aperitivi* are held in many coffee bars and restaurants before the Italian dinner hour. They are widespread in Italian cities such as

Florence and Milan. Accompanying snacks may simply include char-cuterie, but should you find an excellent *aperitivo*, you can satisfy your hunger with an assortment of rice salads, pasta dishes, meats, cheeses, and vegetables, among other items. While prices can vary depending on your choice of beverage, the city and locale, for around €10-15, you can enjoy what I'd call a chic Italian mini buffet. Look for an *aperitivo* to start around an hour or two prior to the dinner hour, often between 5:30-7:00 pm.

Cafes in Italy

In urban areas, you'll find at least one café or coffee shop in every neighborhood. With a long counter for patrons and an industrial espresso machine, you can't miss them. Although known in Italy as a *bar*, they are not where Italians go for drinking alcohol as an activity. Understanding how the *bar* works will take you far, so I will go into depth on this subject. Bars have a social function and are a place to get a *panino, gelato, caffè* (coffee), or enjoy a casual drink among friends. At the start of the day, these cafes are part of many Italians' morning routines. Breakfast dishes common in Anglo-Saxon and North American countries, including cereals, meats, bacon, eggs, or pancakes, are not traditionally on the menu. Instead, most Italians will have a coffee with a pastry or a croissant, if they eat anything at all.

Bars are incredibly convenient, holding continuous hours, usually open from 7:30 am-8 pm. You can buy a sandwich or snack outside the standard Italian meal timetable. Some bars may even function as a pared-down restaurant with a few daily specials. I recall being on business, staying near a train station with mostly ethnic restaurants. But I wanted a light snack to go, or *da portare via* in Italian. I found a typical Italian bar and asked if they could prepare something other than a panino. Maybe mozzarella, cold cuts, and some vegetables...no problem. I was out the door in a few minutes, parcel in hand. Use your judgment and gauge the situation.

There are approximately 150,000 establishments classified as bars in Italy, and the majority are independently owned. You'll find that not all bars are created equal; they have varying levels of quality, service, prices, and offerings. You may need to be careful of bars in tourist areas and near the center of popular destinations. I learned this the hard way while leading a summer study abroad program in Firenze (Florence). Before meeting my students for a tour of the world-renowned *Uffizi* galleries I was in a hurry and opted for the convenience of eating near the Ponte Vecchio, a historic bridge lined with charming medieval buildings, jewelry shops, and street performers—and a crowded tourist site. Attempting to get a healthier lunch, I entered a bar and asked for a *panino al tonno* (tuna sandwich). In the middle of our tour, I became so ill that an ambulance came to pick me up. I later found out that the bar didn't refrigerate tuna after opening it and when tuna fish spoils, it develops histamines, mimicking an allergic reaction that could be fatal.

Italian bars function similarly, although there are differences in how they operate in a busy city or a smaller town. As in most Italian food shops, it's presumed that if you've entered, you've already decided what you will order. If you need some time, that's okay. You can say *"non ho ancora deciso"* (I haven't decided yet). In busy times, like the morning coffee rush, it will seem like a revolving door of patrons, quickly downing a shot of espresso while they eat a pastry and are on their way. In larger cities, you should approach the cash register first to give the clerk your order and pay. You might say something like *"un panino con cotto, un'acqua gassata, e un caffé, per favore"* (a ham sandwich, sparkling water, and a coffee, please). Next, you bring your receipt to the barista, reiterating your order. If you ordered a *panino*, the barista might ask, *"Te lo/glielo scaldo?"* (Do you want it heated up?) The barista will take your receipt and rip it, returning it to you if you ordered a coffee. At the end of the meal, you will return it to the barista to claim your coffee. In a smaller town with greater trust, you will tell the barista, usually the cashier, your order directly and get your food or drink before paying. If you're unsure whether to pay first or order first, take a few minutes and observe what is happening around you before making a move. Careful observation abroad is a good practice when new to a situation.

Most customers eat and drink their espresso while standing at the counter, where you won't find any seats. There may be a *servizio al tavolo* (table service) in the bar, which could be surprisingly expensive. *Caffè* at the counter is around €1. If you sit down, a server will bring your order. Depending on the bar, this could cost more than €5. You might happily pay extra after hours of walking under the sweltering Italian summer sun. A bar can be the perfect location to give your feet a rest and relax in a comfortable, air-conditioned environment. Just don't sit down unless you are prepared to pay. In areas with heavy tourist traffic, like Piazza San Marco in Venice, you might even pay €10 for an espresso at a table. But wandering farther away to a side street, you'll find the prices drop drastically and the environment is more authentic. Note that coffee is covered extensively later in this chapter.

Paninoteca

Panino is the Italian word for sandwich. *Panini* is the plural form, even though the English-speaking world uses this form to mean one sandwich. These shops can be quick and very high quality. Traditionally, Italian sandwiches are meat and bread or along the lines of tomato, mozzarella, and basil. In recent years, the panino food scene has become quite chic. In trendy areas, you'll find *paninoteca* shops specializing in innumerable, unique combinations that add toppings like gorgonzola cream, mushrooms, broccoli rabe, onion jam, etc. Usually, they will have a few tables for customers, or you can take yours to go.

Gelateria

Famous across the globe, this does not need much explanation. Gelato is the perfect accompaniment to an evening *passeggiata* (stroll, see chapter I). Flavors may be different from what you're used to. Knowing some basic vocabulary is helpful. *Potrei assaggiare* (may

I taste) is a useful phrase. When selecting a gelateria, I'd look for an indication that it is *produzione propria,* meaning they make it on-site. A sign of subpar gelato is if it seems artificial or is hidden under fruit that is deceptively placed on top. This likely means that it was probably made with inferior or artificial ingredients. And, if it's right next to a souvenir shop, I'd probably go somewhere else.

RISTORANTE, TRATTORIA, AND OSTERIA

Beyond the speedier and more budget-friendly options, there are common categories of eateries that shouldn't be missed. Note that while establishments are typically named for the type of service, the lines can blur. For example, when my exhausted toddler needed food and a break on one trip to Italy, in desperation I walked into a bar that had a few tables. I expected to get a quick, mediocre meal. Ultimately, it was phenomenal fare and more like a traditional Italian *trattoria* than a bar. The owner was Sicilian, and the cook was actually from Pakistan. I liked it so much that I brought thirty students there for a farewell dinner. Although restaurants may be inconspicuous at first glance, examining the menu or peeking around inside can help demystify the type of meal and service you can expect.

Ristorante

Italians refer to eating out as *andiamo al ristorante* (let's go to a restaurant). But as a category, *un ristorante* has a different and deliberate meaning that is linked to the expectations of its clientele, especially when compared to a *trattoria.* The difference between *un ristorante* and more informal eateries, such as a *trattoria,* is related to the level of service, atmosphere, ingredients, and prices. Restaurants are more formal establishments, fully staffed. You may notice white tablecloths, a sommelier, and pricey entrees. The fare could be local to the area, or the chef may specialize in fish or meats, ethnic foods, gourmet dishes, or unique offerings that you might not find in the region.

Trattoria

A *trattoria* is usually a family-operated restaurant that serves in a home-cooked style. They tend to be unpretentious neighborhood hangouts. A *trattoria* serves dishes from the area along with regional wines that are brought to the table in a small carafe. Generally speaking, the fare is more moderately priced than at a *ristorante*. One of the charming characteristics of a *trattoria* is the presentation of the offerings. I've been in spots that jot down the daily offerings on paper, crossing them off when they run out. Or you might see them written outside on a chalkboard. These spots are fairly easy to pick out, as they typically have *trattoria* on the signage. Another giveaway is if the décor could be a hodgepodge of mementos or appears quite simple.

Osteria

Traditionally, an *osteria* was known as a simpler establishment that also functioned as an inn, where patrons could expect a room and wine accompanied by a little food. Its meaning has evolved. Today, you shouldn't expect them to offer a place to sleep, and the term could be interchangeable with *trattoria*. In theory, it should focus more on drinks than food. An *osteria* might be a wine or tapas bar or more akin to an elegant *trattoria*. If you want a substantial meal, explore its menu and atmosphere before choosing this option.

MEAL TIMES

Restaurants are not open all day long (except bars/cafes). Mealtimes may vary slightly but are generally listed below:

Colazione, breakfast 7:30-10:00 am (held at a bar/cafe, not at restaurants)

Pranzo, lunch 12:30-3:30 pm/12:30-15:30

Cena, dinner 7:30-10:30 pm/19:30-22.30

WHAT TO EXPECT AT A TABLE SERVICE EATERY

As if a character in a fairytale, you'll meander Italy's quaint cobblestone streets with curiosity and will be drawn to some enchanting locale. Perhaps a *ristorante, trattoria, osteria,* or *pizzeria* juts out just around the corner. Your eye will catch the facade's poetically decaying stucco exposing medieval bricks underneath. The aroma of *soffritto* (sautéed herbs, carrots, onions, and celery) and sauces wafts out the door, pulling you in. As soon as you enter, you will be greeted. Maybe. Don't expect a perky host to say, *"Welcome to Mario's! How many are in your party?"* Instead, some guy, probably a waiter carrying dishes, will look up at you and say, *"sì?"* At that point, you'll indicate that you'd like to eat, ask if there is room, and tell him how many are in your group. So far, so good.

You'll be escorted to a table that could be inches away from another diner. And unlike the American practice, waitpersons will not introduce themselves. Occasionally, you might be asked if you want to see a menu. I'm not sure why customers are asked this. Perhaps it's because entrees are sometimes listed on a menu board outside. On the menu, you'll notice offerings listed in an à la carte format: pastas, vegetables, soups, meats, and desserts, rather than lunch or dinner as a combination plate. You may often see predetermined meal menus that include several course meals for a fixed price. Italians typically eat meals in courses, selecting a few items individually. The courses have a particular order. However, not all are commonly ordered unless it's a formal occasion or celebration. It's common to order a *primo* and *secondo* in a restaurant. While the below are not explicitly courses, this is the order food is consumed in a traditional long-form Italian meal.

- *Antipasto,* appetizer (might include sliced meats, toasts, cheeses, pâtés)
- *Primo,* pasta, rice dishes, polenta or soup
- *Secondo,* meat or fish served with a *contorno,* vegetables or potatoes

- *Insalata,* salad (usually comes plain with carafes of olive oil and vinegar)
- *Formaggio,* cheese and *frutta,* fruit
- *Dolce,* dessert
- *Caffè,* coffee (served after the meal and dessert are completed)

After you've had time to review the menu, the waiter will return and say *"Dimmi"* or *"Mi dica"* (tell me, depending on the informal or formal form). Or you might be asked whether you've decided (*"Ha deciso?"* or *"Avete deciso?"*, singular or plural forms). You can reply, *"Prendo"* (I'll have) and list the items. Or, if in a group, you might say *"per me"* and the food or drink. For example, *"Per me una pizza."* The *per me* means I'll have a pizza. Either way, make sure to follow the request with *per favore* (please). Another version might be *da bere* (to drink) or *da mangiare* (to eat). Again, you can use *prendo* to indicate what you will have. *Prendo* literally translates to "I take," and it works for food and drinks.

Coffee is consumed after dessert. If you want them together, you will need to ask. Years ago, during a large lunch gathering at my aunt Sara's home, I recall slowly savoring a piece of cake, anticipating that it would pair wonderfully with the fragrant espresso that had just percolated from the stovetop *moka* pot. As aunt Sara cleared the dishes, she kept peering back to check to see if I had finished my cake. After a few minutes, I relented and ate the last bits. Poof, like magic, she appeared with a tray of espresso cups. While this may sound like some draconian custom, she thought the polite thing to do was not rush my dessert by bringing out the coffee.

Portions tend to be smaller than what you might expect at home. For lunch, it's common to order a *primo, secondo,* and *contorno* or *insalata,* while dinner, traditionally, is much lighter and may be a bowl of soup or cold cuts with some bread and fruit. But, when dining out, Italians deviate from this practice and take the opportunity to try a variety of foods. As soon as the kitchen finishes preparing your plate, it's delivered. Rarely will a server wait to bring everyone's food simultaneously. So rather than allow the meal to get cold, say *"Buon appetito!"* (Enjoy your meal) to your dining companions. This signals that it's okay for them to dig in while the meal is still hot. Nearly everything should be eaten with a utensil except for a roll, which can be torn. Fruit is typically peeled and cut at the table, and cheese can be eaten with a fork. Italians do not switch hands when cutting food with a knife and fork. By the way, using the side of your fork to cut your food is not typical. And when you aren't using a utensil, you set it down, positioning the surface that comes in contact with your food on the side of your plate while its handle rests on the table. Usually, no salt, pepper, butter (even for bread), parmesan, hot pepper flakes, or olive oil (except with salad) will be at your table. It would be unexpected and potentially rude to ask for these condiments, as the chef is the expert and knows best. While it can be perceived as impolite to modify how a chef prepares your meal, I've had success ordering off-menu at smaller restaurants and less busy locations.

During one drizzly spring afternoon in the mountainous Aosta region, I entered Ristorante Casa Ciuca. It seemed like the perfect day for a hot bowl of soup, which was not listed on the menu. So in the humblest way I could, I just asked, saying something like, *"Avete per caso un po' di minestra di verdure?"* (Any chance you have some vegetable soup?) Guess what? In twenty minutes, they brought out a steaming bowl with a side of crusty bread and an abundance of grated Parmigiano to sprinkle over it.

Cheese is taboo on any seafood, yet Italians will have tuna on pizza or shrimp added to pesto sauce. (Occasionally Italians forget, and I once saw my uncle get shamed for requesting it.) As you might expect, pasta is quite popular, and some Italians eat it nearly daily. Locals do not cut their pasta, slurp hanging strands, or twirl it with a spoon. They neatly and efficiently position it on a fork and use the side of the dish to twist it into manageable bites.

Once your dish has arrived, don't expect your waiter to return often to refill drinks or ask how you like your meal. If you need a server, you should make eye contact and gesture. Slightly motion with your hand and say *scusi* (pardon me). Italians are not in the habit of telling the waiter if they don't like the meal or sending food back. This could insult the chef, who may be the owner or the owner's husband, wife, sister, etc. You might want to approach dining out as being at a friend's house for dinner. If you wouldn't express displeasure with their cooking, you probably shouldn't in Italy.

You will not find tall glasses of water filled with ice at the table, although Italians consume ice in beverages if it is an oppressively hot summer day. Restaurants do not serve tap water. If you want water with your meal, you must order a bottle. Diners share large water bottles, as you would a bottle of wine. While eating at a restaurant, you'll most commonly observe that Italians drink water, Coca-Cola (young people), or wine. Pairing pizza with beer or Coca-Cola is customary, but your typical Italian would not order wine with pizza.

"ITALIAN" FOODS YOU WON'T FIND IN ITALY

If you grew up outside of Italy, you could have some misperceptions of Italian food. It might be different in your home country for a variety of reasons. The absence of Italy's Mediterranean climate altered the type of ingredients available. Italian immigrants who fled poverty decades ago found greater abundance abroad and added meat to sauces. Or inventive Italian immigrants created Italian-themed dishes, or traditions evolved. These examples provide an idea of some of the things you won't find in Italy: chicken or veal parmesan, Italian subs, manicotti, spaghetti and meatballs, fettuccine alfredo, chicken over pasta, garlic bread, fluffy breadsticks, pepperoni pizza (or pineapple on pizza for that matter), and even "Italian" salad dressing. An Italian friend once said, "If you see an Italian flag on the logo of a food in the US, I can guarantee you that it is not Italian."

Il Conto

At a sit-down eatery with table service, such as a *pizzeria, ristorante, trattoria,* or *osteria,* the bill will not arrive as soon as you are finished. Italians take time to enjoy their meals and company. Thus, it is impolite to rush patrons out the door. If you don't speak up or begin to leave, your bill might not arrive until you decide to walk out the door (I don't recommend that). To get the check, calmly make eye contact and gesture to the waiter. Politely say, *"il conto, per favore"* (the check, please). Occasionally, your waiter might have disappeared. In that case, you can walk up to the cash register or gesture for another employee. You should also be aware that splitting the check is not always common. You can ask if it's possible. But be prepared to work this out when sharing a meal with friends. In some more informal formal eateries, diners go to the register and list what they ate, and it becomes a non-issue.

Tipping

Most restaurants in Italy have a *coperto* (service charge for bread and sitting down). So, you shouldn't expect to tip according to percentages; each customer already pays the mandatory *coperto* that will be included in the final bill. At the end of the meal, you may want to leave two or three euro total (not per person) on the table. An acceptable maximum that might be added for a more expensive meal is 5 to 15 percent.

How to Avoid a Tourist Trap

As a frequent visitor to travel forums, a common question is, "Does anyone have recommendations for a good restaurant in the center of Rome?" Suggestions can be helpful, presuming who you ask is credible. But it's much more fun to make your own adventure than relive someone else's trip. You will learn from it even if it's not an ideal experience. Instead of a list of places to eat, knowing what to look for is better. The quality of Italian food is consistently high. However, lower-quality restaurants can be problematic in tourist areas, or you may be charged twice as much. To avoid tourist traps, avoid eateries that have the below characteristics:

- Their menu is translated into multiple languages and prominently displayed outside.
- They are promoting a tourist menu.
- You're solicited as you walk by, usually in English.
- "No cover charge" is advertised.
- Loads of tourists are dining there.
- It's located right across from souvenir shops.
- The restaurant is open outside of traditional meal hours.
- It doesn't close between meals (continuous service from lunch to dinner).
- As part of the service, they offer patrons complimentary limoncello.
- There is an entertainer playing the accordion or singing.
- An example of the food is displayed in a case outside.
- The menu displays dozens of photos of the food.
- The menu is multiple pages long.

Even menus that have translations can be suspect. One sunny afternoon in Rome, I strolled through Piazza Navona with a friend who was in town to study architecture. In the mood for lunch, we stopped at an open restaurant during off-peak hours. As I looked over the English-language menu the waiter gave us, I noticed that below the pizzas was an asterisk with the word *surgelato*. While the entire menu included translations, there was this one Italian word. *Surgelato* means "frozen." This was likely included as an Italian would not tolerate a frozen pizza, but tourists might not know any better. Remember the above tips to have a better, more authentic dining experience. If Italian workers or businesspeople are inside during their lunch break, it's a good sign. To really step up your game, check out the Italian guide and app produced by the Slow Food organization, *Osterie d'Italia*, which lists hundreds of reviewed and acclaimed *trattorie, osterie, agriturismi* and *ristoranti* that promote the local food heritage. It goes so far as to even recommend the locale's specialties, gluten-free, and vegetarian dishes. You can also reference the *Gambero Rosso* guides that also cover categories such as bars, bakeries, pastry shops, and street food. On the app TheFork, you can see customer ratings and make reservations.

Coffee

Coffee is much more than a boost of caffeine to Italians. Having an espresso is a shared ritual that is ingrained into the boot-shaped country's national heritage. A beverage that is consumed by the majority of adults, it has an undeniable social role, creating an opportunity for friends and community members to catch up and connect on the issues of the day. Often instead of asking, *"Non ti va di fare un giro?"* (Do you feel like going for a stroll/ride?) One might suggest, *"Andiamo a prenderci un caffè?"* (Meaning, why don't we get a coffee?) But it's really a metaphor for let's do something together. After dinner and lunch, it's a way to spend time together and is offered to guests. Typically, if someone is invited into an Italian home, the first thing asked is whether you want a coffee. Getting a coffee is also seen as an opportunity to take a short break, even just for a few minutes. In the morning, most Italians consider it indispensable for the aroma that fills their homes and as a pick-me-up.

I spoke with Martina Mazzoleni about the significance of coffee to Italians. She's the coffee shop and marketing manager for Caffè Ernani, Milan's historic *torrefazione* (coffee roaster). Caffè Ernani has a coffee shop in Corso Buenos Aires, in the heart of a bustling Milanese shopping district. Martina said the meaning of a coffee depends on the time of day. An Italian bar is a *punto di ritrovo*, a hangout. They symbolize relationships. Italians typically frequent the same bar, have a rapport with the barista, and feel at home. An Italian's *bar di fiducia* (regular coffee bar) is a place to relax and recharge for the rest of your day. Italians generally have two *bar di fiducia*, one near home and one near the office. Once you're a regular, it's a gathering place for social interactions, whether with friends or just the barista, who knows your name, what you order, and who you are. Choosing the right bar can be a little like dating. You frequent a few and decide which one makes coffee to your liking and which barista you connect best with.

Italian coffee is a family tradition, especially regarding the *moka*, a stovetop coffee maker that produces coffee akin to espresso. A *moka* is an Italian icon and has been around for almost one hundred years. The *moka* was invented by Alfonso Bialetti, which explains Bialetti's success as one of the world's most popular brands of *moka*. It's simple yet makes excellent, strong coffee. Because a *moka* boils water, while true espresso is extracted at a lower temperature, the coffee that comes out of it isn't technically espresso. If you book an Airbnb or stay in an Italian home, you will likely find a *moka* pot. Fill the bottom chamber with water (preferably room temperature or warmer) up to the steam valve (you'll see a little nut inside). Then, place the filter in and add finely ground coffee equal to the filter's height. Pushing it down with your hand or adding excess coffee will pack it too densely. This will cause it to take too long to extract and taste burnt. Next, tightly screw on the top pitcher. It should be heated on the stove at a medium to medium high setting. If the plastic handle is at the edge of the burner, you'll melt it, so position it over the edge. Once nearly half of the coffee has filled the top pitcher, you can shut off the burner. Try it as many Italians do in the morning for breakfast, in a caffè latte. Just fill a mug with espresso and warm milk.

Unlike stopping at Starbucks, espresso at an Italian bar comes without frills. Outside of Italy, different chains or independently owned shops often have their own version of a latte, cappuccino, and espresso, which come in all different sizes. Even though most

Italian bars are independently owned, the coffee menu, how it is ordered, and how Italians consume it are nearly identical. In the following section, I will provide some details on two major preparations that tend to be the most popular among Italians, *un caffè* (an espresso shot) and *un cappuccino*, as well as mention a few other popular options.

Un Caffè

When you order *un caffè* (a coffee), by default, you will get an espresso (pronounced *eh-spress-o,* note there is no x sound in the word). When ordering a coffee, you can say *"Un caffè per favore"* (a coffee please), or substitute in the name of any drink you are ordering. Italian espresso is less than an ounce of concentrated black coffee. In contrast, the American version of espresso is usually more voluminous. In an Italian bar, no one will ask if you want room for cream, a *doppio* (double espresso), or if it's for here or to-go. With Covid-19, when everything was only to go, the takeaway concept has changed slightly. But asking for an espresso to go typically would strike Italians as odd for a few reasons. First off, it's one ounce. Are you really going to carry it around with you and drink it later? Second, Italian espresso is high quality, but it starts to lose its luster after a few minutes. Espresso is intended to be consumed as a shot. Finally, Italians appreciate enjoying a moment's break in the day. Having a coffee in a bar is not only a necessary pick-me-up, it can also be a social occasion and a refuge from outside chaos. In Italy, espresso and many other beverages are consumed while you stand at the counter, known as *al banco*. After finishing an espresso, asking for *"un bicchiere d'acqua per favore"* (a glass of water please) is standard. The barista will take out a small glass and pour you some *gassata* or *naturale* (sparkling or flat), depending on your preference. Occasionally, it's on the house. Other times they may add thirty or forty cents to the bill.

There are some differences in coffee preparation throughout Italy. In the north, arabica is more popular, so coffee tends to be more delicate and acidic. It is served in a warm ceramic cup. Regardless of the type of cup, it will always have a saucer. For an Italian, coffee seems better when served on a saucer because it's ingrained in the psychology of taking a coffee break. As you move to central Italy, espresso may have more robusta mixed in and will often be presented in a glass cup. In the south and Naples you'll find that the espresso is made from robusta beans. It is strong and served exclusively in a scalding hot ceramic cup. Naples takes espresso very seriously. One uniquely Neapolitan tradition is the idea of a *caffè sospeso*. When a client buys a coffee, they often pay for two, so those without the means to pay can have one for free.

Cappuccino

Cappuccino (or *cappuccio* around Milan and Torino) is an inseparable part of the Italian breakfast menu. Baristas serve cappuccino warm instead of scalding hot. It's made with about four ounces (125 ml) of milk, less than you may find outside of Italy, but shops worldwide vary. It has nearly half the volume of an American cappuccino. Generally, it's made with whole milk. Almond, soy, or skim milk are not as common in coffee bars, and Italians don't typically drink milk after the breakfast hour. Ordering a cappuccino later in the day is viewed suspiciously. Having one after a meal is not an Italian custom and is a practice that will peg you as a tourist. Regarding cappuccino, Italian author Beppe Severgnini quipped, "After ten o'clock in the morning, it is unethical, and possible even unlawful, to order one. You won't have one in the afternoon unless the weather is very cold." [2] As is the case with espresso, cappuccino is served in ceramic cups, and it will not typically be offered to go. Exceptions are in larger cities, at American chains, or some train stations.

While you probably won't find an iced caramel macchiato in Italy, there are plenty of options to get your coffee fix. Here is a

---

[2] Beppe Severgnini. *La Bella Figura: A field guide to the Italian mind.* (New York: Broadway Books, 2006).

summary of the most common preparations:

- *un caffè,* just under an ounce (30 ml) of espresso.
- *un caffè americano,* an espresso with hot water added (or a pitcher of water served alongside for you to mix yourself).
- *un caffè corretto,* just under an ounce (30 ml) of espresso, with a small amount of *grappa* or other liquor.
- *un caffè lungo,* an espresso with a bit more water added.
- *un caffè macchiato,* an espresso with a few drops of steamed milk on top.
- *un caffè shakerato, un caffè lungo* shaken with ice and sugar.
- *un cappuccino,* an espresso with four ounces (125 ml) of steamed milk and froth.
- *un latte macchiato,* like a cappuccino but with more milk and less froth.
- *un marocchino,* popular with many Italian youths, is like a mini mocha or mini cappuccino with the addition of chocolate.

Culturally speaking, the Italian coffee bar can be a gem. Well-dressed senior citizens sprawl out their newspapers on tables, elegant men and women grab a quick shot and greet baristas as old friends, and children stop in on their way to and from school for a *cornetto* or ice cream bar. If you're in the same area for several days, I encourage you to try a few bars, each with a different vibe. The baristas are often there on a daily basis and will get to know you even as a visitor. During off-peak hours, you can strike up a conversation or learn about the area. I always tell my students to use the excuse of making a purchase to engage in chit-chat and practice speaking Italian. Broadly speaking, Italians are interested in meeting new people and will ask you about yourself. They may be more guarded in tourist hotspots, but venturing farther out is a fun way to immerse yourself more deeply.

Another feature of a bar is that they have a restroom for customers' use. Walking into an independently owned shop without buying something and asking to use the bathroom could be rude. You might even be told outright it is for customers. However, make a purchase, even something inexpensive, then ask. You could simply ask to buy *un bicchiere d'acqua* (a glass of water) to drink at the bar, which will be poured from a bottle and will likely be 30-70 cents. Then, ask *"Dov'è il bagno?"* (Where is the bathroom?).

Note that lunch and dinner may be an hour earlier in northern Italy and the Italian-speaking canton of Ticino, Switzerland. Times could skew later during summer months, particularly further south.

Grocery Shopping

"I go every day," my Italian friend told me when asked how often he buys groceries. Italians commonly visit markets, small shops, and bakeries at least several days a week. This differs from how food is typically purchased in the US and UK, where the supermarket is frequented less often and primarily for nonperishable, dry goods. The majority of Italians live in urban centers and incorporate their neighborhood's *botteghe* (smaller specialized shops) into their daily routine, as they pay close attention to the quality of what they eat. Here is a listing of a few common shops you will encounter.

> *Alimentari,* small neighborhood grocery store with a limited selection of products (see Alimentari section below).
> *Forno, panetteria, panettiere* or *fornaio,* a bakery with assorted breads, cookies, sweets, and pizzas.
> *Salumeria,* a delicatessen that specializes in cooked, cured, or smoked meats, commonly made of pork, and some

cheeses.

Fruttivendolo or negozio di frutta e verdura, a fruit and vegetable store or stand.

Macelleria, a butcher shop that may have some cured meats, sauces, olive oil, and other staples.

Pasticceria, a fancier sweets shop with cakes and the kind of small artisan pastries you might bring to a dinner party.

Pescheria, a fish store that may have both fresh and frozen products.

While farmers markets, eating locally, and paying attention to the seasonality of foods have become trendy concepts in the US and the UK, in Italy, the idea of eating fruits and vegetables when they're in season, at the peak of ripeness, is an age-old idea. It's built into the Italian routine and harvest festivals that celebrate chestnuts, pumpkins, truffles, and more, punctuate the Italian fresh and local food ideology. Italians intimately know their foods, often down to the producer and its territorial origins and are particularly proud of products from their regions. Bread, cheeses, and meats often contain fewer preservatives compared to products you find in the US–after a day, that *sfilatino* (Italian baguette) roll you purchased with a beautiful crusty outside and soft center is so hard you might break a tooth. Perishable items don't tend to keep for more than a few days, so buying large quantities can lead to rotten and wasted foods. Consequentially, you may observe that Italian homes have smaller refrigerators than in your home country.

MERCATO

Visiting a food market, known as the *mercato,* is a sensory journey. The stalls are bursting with crates of fragrant seasonal produce, with prices marked on smartly placed handwritten signs. Around the time that purple wisteria, warmly hued tulips, and violets begin to color the landscape, fresh asparagus, fava beans, and spinach that have been plucked from the earth appear in abundance. During a summer visit, expect to see bright orange zucchini flowers that work their way into a variety of dishes; scarlet tomatoes; and plump cherries and apricots, just a sliver of the spectrum of colorful fruits you'll find. And when the autumn brings crisp mornings, your eyes will catch rotund porcini mushrooms, deep brown chestnuts, and dark leafy greens. While at a winter market, a wide range of cabbages and hearty vegetables, such as fennel, appear. Throughout the year, the aromas are intoxicating: massive loaves of bread; Nocellara and Bella di Cerignola olives, along with scores of other varieties from Sicily, Puglia, and Calabria; freshly cut pecorino, Grana Padano, and *caciocavallo* cheeses are just part of the *formaggio* (cheese) on display behind glass cases; and piping hot, succulent, roasting chickens entice passersby. Bargain hunters haggle with spirited vendors, who compete as they shout out their prices. Usually, they're a deal compared to those in the supermarket.

You should arrive at markets early. By the lunch hour, the ones that popped up in the early morning are empty. In place of the patrons who crowded the streets are opportunistic pigeons scavenging a mess of empty cartons and papers for scraps of food. Larger cities often have smaller markets every weekday, and sometimes there are indoor venues. They alternate by neighborhood during the week, and there's usually a large market in every decent-sized town on the weekends.

As a customer, you shouldn't handle the produce directly. Instead, indicate what you would like and the vendor will select it for you. You'll order some products by quantity and others by weight. Italians use the metric system; if you're accustomed to ounces and pounds, you'll have to learn to order in hectograms or 100-gram units. In Italian, they are known as *etti*.

1 *etto* = ¼ lb (0.22 lbs)
2 *etti* = ½ lb (0.44 lbs)
4 *etti* = 1 lb (0.88 lbs)
5 *etti* = ½ kilo (kg) = 1 lb (1.1 lbs) or *mezzo chilo*
10 *etti* = 1 kilo (kg) = 2 lbs (2.2 lbs) or *un chilo*

If you forget the translation and conversions, you can purchase by the number of units. For meats and cheeses, ask for *fette* (slices). At a minimum, know how to say the numbers one through ten in Italian. If necessary, you can communicate the quantity with your fingers. But use it as an opportunity to learn food vocabulary words and to understand how much your order weighs. Next time, try the same order in *etti* or the appropriate Italian quantity.

Items for sale may be listed in kilo or *etti* so be careful. At the market or grocery store, you may see Prosciutto di Parma listed at 3,30 *all'etto* or 30,30 *al kg*. A side note on *etti* relates to restaurants where I've seen fish listed on the menu by the *etto* but sold as a whole fish, which might end up being 5 or 10 times the amount listed in *etti*. So before ordering, make sure you understand how you could be charged.

Back to quantities, sometimes it's more logical to order a bit less precisely. As you spend time in markets, you will hear Italians using these words when ordering.

un po'	a little
un pezzo	a piece
più piccolo, più grande	smaller, larger
troppo	too much
di meno	less
di più	more
per una (due…) persona(e)	for one (two…) people
locale/nostrano	locally made

In the vocabulary above, I intentionally included *locale/nostrano*. I'll provide some examples of why this can be useful. While Italy's Prosciutto di Parma is well known, other regions also make prosciutto. It might be worth trying and less expensive. There are countless cheese varieties in Italy, so asking for *formaggio locale* will likely get you something fresh and can be a fun way to try something new.

ALIMENTARI

Supermarkets and small *alimentari* (corner stores) are convenient and may offer a calmer experience. The *alimentari* are typically small "mom and pop" shops with a limited selection. Usually, you will find bottled drinks, wine, bread, olive oil, cooked and cured meats, pastas, fruits, vegetables, and dry goods such as toilet paper and paper towels. Beyond the staples, there is not a standard slate of items. Some products will be displayed behind the counter, and the shopkeeper will have to retrieve them from a storeroom. The shopkeeper will likely engage with you if you can't locate what you need in a few moments. For language learners, *alimentari* can be a great asset. They provide a low-pressure environment to practice Italian, often with a benign *nonna* (Italian grandmother) who likely will interrogate you. *Nonna* might as well work for the FBI. If you return a few times, she'll understand your eating habits, know where you are from, why you are in Italy, where you live, and whether you have a significant other. Your trips to her shop might be like visiting a motherly old friend who offers counsel on nutrition and recipes. A phenomenon in Italy is that *nonna* and other shopkeepers can replicate the Italian version of a Subway sandwich shop. If a small shop sells rolls and sliced meat, the worker will happily cut just enough *prosciutto, salame* or *mortadella* along with a thick hunk of aged Italian cheese to make you a sandwich, calculating an exact price. What you won't find are condiments or the use of items like pickles or lettuce, so sandwiches may be dry. While not advertised, this is an off-menu trick that is incredibly useful.

Italy offers so much to take in. An inexpensive, quick sandwich, some fruit, and a hunk of cheese are ideal for days when you prefer exploring rather than spending time in a restaurant for a long lunch. To ask about this, you will say, *"Si fanno i panini?"* (Are sandwiches made here?) or *"Mi può fare un panino?"* (Can you make me a sandwich?).

As quaint as an *alimentari* can be, it will be costlier than a supermarket, and Italian shopkeepers have a magical charm that almost makes you feel guilty if you don't buy more. If you come in for just a liter of water, before you can leave, they will say, *"Niente frutta... ti serve la pasta...altro?"* (Any fruit...do you need pasta... anything else?). *Nonna* shares a trait common among Italian vendors: she is not only a charmer, but somehow she makes it seem like she is doing you a favor. To not disappoint her, you could walk out having spent €50 on all kinds of things she suggested.

IL SUPERMERCATO

Supermarkets are the least intimidating place to buy food, as no shopkeeper will approach you. Be mindful of the operating hours. In smaller cities, stores may close on Sundays or for a few hours over lunch. When located in the city center, they tend to be small or medium-sized shops with the large markets at the perimeter or in a shopping center. Supermarkets are a great place to begin learning about the culture. You should take some time to look around, understand what locals are buying and observe the behaviors of the people in the store. The supermarket will generally share many similarities with what you're used to, but a few things may strike you as odd. In Italy, UHT (shelf-stable milk) is widespread. Eggs, including pheasant and other speckled varieties, are kept at room temperature. You may notice a much smaller or nonexistent selection of ethnic foods. This includes items from your home country, which could consist of peanut butter, tacos, American cheese, maple syrup, Asian sauces, etc. In the past, my students expressed frustration with the puny size of the cereal aisle in an Italian store; the same could be felt by Italians looking for cheese or pasta in an American grocery store.

As opposed to a market stall environment with vendors, at the supermarket, when you select fresh produce, you must wear disposable plastic gloves that are provided for hygienic reasons. Even before the global coronavirus pandemic, shoppers followed this practice. Near the produce, there are scales to weigh and print out a price label that you stick on the items before you proceed to the cash register. If you skip this step, the cashier will make you get out of line to weigh the items. As the cashier scans your items, they ask, *"Vuoi un sachetto/una busta?"* (Do you want a bag?) In Italy, you will be charged a few cents for each plastic bag you receive. Customers are responsible for bagging their own groceries. It can be convenient to bring a few durable bags with you. A backpack is great if you have a long trek home or plan to carry liters of water or other heavy purchases. Large grocery stores offer shopping carts for customers, but they are typically locked together, and a one-euro coin will be required to access them. When you return your cart to where they are locked up, your coin pops back out.

III

La Bella Figura

The only true source of politeness is consideration.
—WILLIAM GILMORE SIMMS

If you aren't familiar with Italian, *fare una bella figura* means making a good impression. I see it as a foundational concept in Italian behavior. Culturally, it's perceived positively in terms of behavior, dress, hospitality, manners, and displaying a little cultural know-how when appropriate. Manners extend to attempting to speak some Italian and even something as seemingly trivial as putting your feet on a seat.

La bella figura can help explain why Italians don't leave the house looking sloppy, and why they show tremendous hospitality. When I travel to Italy to visit Italian friends and relatives, it's impossible to even think about paying for my coffee, let alone a meal. There's also an element of charm that accompanies this concept. You will likely find yourself beguiled by exceptionally friendly people who make you feel like you're the center of the universe. It's important to recognize what is happening and enjoy it in these circumstances. As a relationship develops, some initial gushing may wane. Still, the principle of the *bella figura* will continue to be strong. Keep an eye out for it. Replicating some of the behaviors will gain you respect.

Particularly when invited to someone's home, gift giving can make *una bellissima figura*. However, a small gift will be greatly appreciated as a token of friendship or gratitude. Gifts are packaged with tremendous care. In fact, I've never received a gift in Italy that wasn't tastefully wrapped. If you purchase something intended as a present, the clerk will usually ask if you'd like it wrapped. Even without asking, this often happens by default, extending to pastries or fresh gnocchi from a bakery that are neatly tied up with a bow. Should you be invited to someone's home, packaged chocolates, pastries, or a regional specialty are good choices. Flowers are also appropriate with a caveat. They should be given only in odd numbers while chrysanthemums are typically reserved for funerals and red roses are associated with romantic relationships. If you have expertise on wine, presenting your host with a high quality bottle can make the right impression. However, if you're unsure, you're better off not to risk bringing an inferior vintage. As an aside, in Italian culture, it is polite to open the gift immediately and express appreciation for it. When in doubt, you can ask the advice of a shopkeeper, letting them know that you want a gift to make *una bella figura*. I've done this before and have gotten excellent suggestions.

Clothing

One of the easiest ways to spot a tourist or student is to look for flip-flops, comfortable athletic shoes, white socks, shorts, sweatshirts, sports T-shirts, and baseball caps or fedoras, which for reasons I cannot understand, many tourists purchase thinking it is ideal for Italian travel. Gianni Marangio, who works with American students at Temple University's Rome campus, mentioned that he can spot them as soon as they get off the plane just by how they dress. Advertising sports teams is a big giveaway, as Italians display them only when at the stadium. Showing off your team colors outside might subject an Italian to harassment from a fan of another team. As a college student, I experienced this when I wore a Bologna soccer shirt in Milan. Additionally, Italian clothes tend not to display large logos or brands and fit more tightly, even for men.

Most Italians would only wear shorts when traveling around

Rome if it were scorching hot in August (when Italians are typically on vacation), at the beach, and during sports activities. Even Italian university students going to class would not wear shorts, flip-flops, or slippers. Flip-flops are only worn at the beach.

As an example of dress, my uncle Sesto was never without a necktie. Although he lived in a small village, no matter where he went, he made an effort to look respectable. Italians pride themselves on impeccable grooming and style. Every time they go out, they are dressed as if it's an occasion (although this does not mean flashy or ostentatious). While some trends are changing in Italy, they typically do not wear sweatpants and generally do not look sloppy. While I don't ascribe to the idea that you should necessarily try to pass yourself off as a local, I think there are advantages to not standing out. If you want to blend in, dress more conservatively, formally, and in nondescript, well-fitting clothes. I opt for neutral, darker colors without prominent logos or writing on T-shirts. While you might not fit in, there's no reason to stand out in an unfamiliar environment.

There are also practical reasons to appear more put together. In Italy, you will not be permitted to enter many churches and some restaurants if you wear tank tops, shorts, or short skirts. For women wearing sleeveless tops, it is a good idea to carry a light shawl or scarf, which you can use to cover your shoulders when entering a church.

Additionally, many people will form opinions about you based on your dress. The level of service you receive may be different based on your appearance. For example, as a student, I recall stopping at a post office after a trip to the gym in my worn-out workout clothes. The clerk eyed me up when I asked to mail a somewhat cumbersome package. Unknowingly, I had made *una brutta figura* (poor impression) and was unceremoniously told that he couldn't do anything with it. Later in the day, I tried the post office again after showering and getting dressed in business casual attire. They took the package without hesitation. I've had similar experiences on how I was treated in stores depending on how I presented myself. I even recall a friend telling me he went to the front of the line in a hospital because he was wearing a suit. While this isn't a universal truth, many people will gauge your status by how you dress and treat you accordingly.

Formality

The Italian language has a formal and informal register, known as the *lei* and *tu* forms. Speaking informally may be perceived as rude or disrespectful. Aside from young people, relatives, and good friends, address everyone with the *lei* form and with formal greetings (discussed further in the next section). With any professional or authority figure, always use the *lei* form and their title. Note that anyone with a university degree (bachelors) can be called *dottore* (masculine) or *dottoressa* (feminine) meaning doctor, as you might call someone with a PhD. The very same titles are used for physicians. When addressing someone in a business or professional setting, use the doctor title or *signore* (mister/sir) *signora* (miss/madam). It is not recommended to use first names until a rapport develops. With professional distance, it is better to stick with titles. Italy even has specific versions for engineers (*ingengnere*), nurses (*infermiere*), and architects (*architetto*). With professions, while there traditionally have been feminine versions, I'm only including the masculine because in contemporary Italian society, the feminine versions can be viewed as inferior, and the masculine versions are accepted. If you can't remember, *signore*, *signora*, and *dottore* are typically acceptable and will demonstrate respect.

If a rapport feels unnecessarily formal, sometimes Italians may ask "*Ci diamo del tu?*" or "*Mi può dare del tu.*" Meaning, "Why don't we switch to the *tu* form?" or "You can speak to me in the *tu* form." Usually, this happens when you are on the same level in a social hierarchy, or the person with authority makes the request to the subordinate person. It can be tricky, and you shouldn't initiate lessening the formality unless you are the senior person. As an MBA student, I was on my way to an interview at an Italian branch of Unilever near Milan and one of the internship contacts picked me up to bring me to the office. He was relatively young, and we were speaking formally on the ride over. After a brief exchange, he said *"Posso darle del tu?"* May I give you the *tu* form? Relieved to dispense with the formality, I happily consented. I opened my mouth and started speaking to him in the informal register. He replied, unintentionally using Robert DeNiro's famous line, *"Dici a me?"* Meaning, "Are you talking to me?" We were the only two in the car, so there was no question I was talking to him, but he wanted to demonstrate his position of power. He was implying that I should continue speaking to him formally even though he was informal. When I was later offered the internship, a few factors, including the awkward exchange, left me with the wrong impression. I politely declined the offer.

Greetings

Greetings are powerful prerequisites in Italy. You shouldn't enter a shop or begin an encounter without one. During one of my trips to Italy, Guido, *il fornaio* (the baker), voiced his frustrations to me about this. With his silver hair and glasses, Guido appeared to be in his sixties and had a quaint shop in the complex where I was renting my Airbnb. We had gotten to know each other, bonding over his long (and unsolicited) explanation of the building's trash and recycling system. A few days later, I ran into Guido again, while he was carrying trash to the designated spot in the building's courtyard. He was dressed in his crisp baker's shirt and a cockeyed black and white checkered cap. In Italian fashion, he didn't hesitate to share his thoughts. This time, it was a rant about German and British tourists. "They come and don't even say good morning. They just start pointing to what they want." While I'm sure this doesn't categorically apply to everyone, Guido must have heard enough to be bothered by it. There's some nuance here, as the type of greeting is critical. *Ciao,* which means hello or goodbye, adorns souvenir shop T-shirts and is ubiquitous, but should be used carefully. It has an informal connotation and can be perceived as disrespectful to elders or in an unfamiliar context. I'd equate it to greeting your doctor with "Hey." *Ciao* is okay among younger people and students or if you are speaking with a child. But formal greetings are more neutral or serious in tone. You can use *salve* to say hello anytime, though it's a more sterile greeting. *Buongiorno* (good morning/good day) is appropriate from the morning until around 3 pm, a bit later in the summer. After the Italian lunch hour, you can switch to *buonasera* (good evening). Getting more technical, *buon pomeriggio* (good afternoon) could be used between 1-5 pm but is less common. When you end an encounter, such as leaving a shop, you can say *salve,* which means hello or goodbye. If you are in doubt, using *salve* for all greetings is safe. *Buongiorno* and *buonasera* are also acceptable when leaving a shop. You could also use *buona giornata* or *buona serata,* which mean, have a good day or evening, respectively.

Asking, "Hi, how are you?" isn't common when entering a shop or running into someone. It's not used as a de facto greeting like in the US with the standard "good" response. Think of "How are you?" in the context of being asked this by a close family member or friend who might expect some information. If you wouldn't expect to get information about what is happening in this person's personal life, just say *buongiorno* or *buonasera*, depending on the time of day. In a similar vein, it's not typical to say hello or nod at those you don't know who you pass in the street. In a smaller town or on a hiking trail, it may be common to give a formal greeting to acknowledge a passerby. One curious exception to this rule is when you are on the same elevator with someone where it's common to say hello.

When you are in Italy long enough to develop personal relationships, or upon meeting Italian relatives (even for the first time), you may be greeted with a kiss on either side of the cheek. This may be an actual kiss, just kissing the air, or lightly touching cheeks. Since Covid-19, some may be more hesitant with this practice. For the most part, this practice is an informal greeting. It occurs across all gender combinations, although it is perhaps less common with men greeting men. There is some variation in regions of Italy. The greeting is initiated by leaning to the right, and barely touching your left cheek to your partner's. If you are unsure whether it's appropriate, follow the lead of the Italian you're meeting. There is also some nuance. Just like shaking hands, you don't do it every time you see someone. It's more common during an unexpected encounter, after a long absence, when parting for the night, leaving on a trip, etc.

Flattery

Italians can have a talent for making you feel special. They find a way to charm you through being truly polite and considerate, especially when they want to avoid making a *brutta figura* (poor impression) in situations where you are a client or have a social connection. Everything seems to be *bello* (beautiful) and they will go out of their way to do a small favor for you. But often, it's so ingrained that it's done purely out of kind consideration. I recall being with my young son in an Acqua e Sapone (this literally translates to water and soap) store, a chain that specializes in personal care and cleaning products. Unprompted, the clerk presented him with a small bag of toys. When I'm treated well, I often say *"è gentilissimo"* or *"molto gentile, grazie,"* which equates to "that's very kind." Another way to make a great impression is to use the conditional tense when making a request *"vorrei"* (I would like) as opposed to *"voglio"* (I want). Be sure to end the request with *"per favore"* (please). It seems basic, but trust me, a little politeness will make a phenomenal impression and may lead to better treatment.

Per favore, Per Piacere, and Per Cortesia

Please, a prerequisite for making *una bella figura*, has a few variations that you will hear in Italy: *per favore, per piacere,* and *per cortesia*. While all are essentially interchangeable, they are used in slightly different situations. *Per favore* is more informal, *per piacere* is slightly more formal, while *per cortesia* is somewhat old fashioned and quite formal. With a friend or family member, it would be odd to use *per cortesia*, but with a shopkeeper or in a professional context, it could come across as elegant, poetic, and earn you some respect for effort.

Scusi vs. Permesso

Invariably you will have to get around people, whether in a crowded street, at a shop, or on public transportation. I've observed tourists misunderstand these two words again and again. *Scusi* means excuse me, but it won't get the attention of an Italian to move out of your way. *Scusi* is used when you bump into someone or approach them to ask a question. *Permesso,* on the other hand, if said confidently in a serious tone, means, "Excuse me so I can get past." The second syllable should be strongly emphasized, per-MEH-so. Pay attention to how the Italians say it when getting off a train, bus, etc. You'll notice that with the right cadence, people part like the Red Sea.

Permesso can also be used to ask permission. Before entering someone's home, bedroom, office, or private space, you should ask *"permesso?"* which might even be accompanied by knocking twice. This happens even if you are standing at the door that your host just answered, and they are expecting you. The response will be *"prego"* ("come in"); further uses are explained in the next section. *Permesso* is also the way to ask "Anybody here?" as if announcing yourself in a shop or location where you don't see anyone.

Prego

Prego is a word that will follow you everywhere. Most Italian textbooks will indicate that it means "you're welcome." It's also frequently used to mean "come this way" (as in a restaurant), "please go ahead of me," "take one" (as in a sample), and "go ahead" (with a request such as to take a picture), or "please feel free to enter."

Smiling

In some cultures, flashing a smile at a stranger you pass on the street can be an expected and polite acknowledgment, or even instinctive. In Italian culture, this practice is uncommon. Aside from greeting someone at a shop or restaurant, a smile directed at an individual you don't know might make others uncomfortable or even invite unwanted attention. Women should know that if you return a smile to an unknown man, it is highly likely he will interpret this as romantic interest, rather than a polite acknowledgement. In this case, if you're not interested in engaging with a stranger, it's better to keep a neutral expression.

Staring

Italians tend to be curious and may stare at you. They may be wondering where you're from and why you are there. Especially if you look different, such as having a lighter complexion or are dressed differently than expected. Visitors to Italy from colder countries might go out in February or March with a T-shirt and no jacket, while Italians would not. I've seen American college students leave their buildings with wet hair, which isn't something an Italian would do. While visiting Abruzzo, my brother and I stopped at my aunt Maria's house for lunch. He had just stepped out of the shower a few minutes earlier and was used to letting his hair air dry. Before we sat down to eat, she looked him over, pulled out a hair dryer, and dried his hair herself. Regarding staring, if you're uncomfortable, staring back at someone may make them aware of what they're doing, and they will likely stop.

Alcohol

Although the legal drinking age is eighteen in Italy, alcohol is highly respected and not abused. It's typical for young Italians to enjoy a beer or have an Aperol Spritz with some food during happy hour or with an *aperitivo*. Still, its consumption is more about the experience than partying. Italians have a negative view of public intoxication. In some countries, Friday or Saturday night public drunkenness may be a social norm. In Italy, it is a disgrace. It may be legal to walk around sucking down a beer, but culturally, it's unacceptable behavior. Use good judgment, and don't overconsume.

Food on the Go

Aside from gelato, it's uncommon to see Italians eating on the go. It's not a cultural norm and is even seen as unhealthy. Walking or driving while eating a slice of pizza or a sandwich or sipping a coffee is uncommon among Italians. Some cities, such as Rome and Florence, have had issues with tourists who create crowds and trash piles as they consume food in the streets. In Florence's Via de' Neri street there tends to be major congestion at the confluence of take-out eateries, including the well-known sandwich shop All'Antico Vinaio and the Gelateria dei Neri (I've found both to be worth the trip). The city has even instituted fines for those who linger outside to eat or drink during peak hours in these popular parts of city centers to deal with the problem. If you see posted signs that eating is prohibited, take notice.

Volume

Because visitors lack the context, they might not realize they are much louder than the cultural norms in Italy. This can be confusing because Italians often yell or have spirited conversations. In fact, you may notice them stepping on each other's words, with constant interruptions to insert their opinions. Italians are generally in tune with their emotions and are not afraid to express themselves theatrically. Yet this verbal jousting often doesn't equate to true anger or rage. The difference for a visitor is the combination of the setting and the use of English. Speakers of another language will naturally stand out. Being loud will only draw more attention.

On public transportation, you may notice an occasional loud cell-phone conversation in Italian. But often, there can be dead silence or conversations are carried out in hushed tones. Many tourists miss the context and have conversations that resonate throughout public spaces like train cars. A good rule of thumb is to observe the context before having loud conversations in public.

Making Comparisons

I've witnessed Italians give many blank stares to tourists when they were boasting about how things are done in their country or when they explain things like, "our cars are much bigger," "we have ice cold air conditioning," "houses are more spacious," and so on. It's natural to think in terms of comparisons. But if it could reflect negatively on the host culture, keep it to yourself. Chances are that they've heard it before. Be mindful of what you are saying to avoid appearing like you are judging your host's society.

IV

Finding Your Peak Experiences

*We must look at the lens through which we see the
world, as well as the world we see, and that the
lens itself shapes how we interpret the world.*
—STEPHEN COVEY

A peak experience is an event that creates a sense of awe, gives you
new insights, and could start you down a path of positive personal
transformation. It has happened to me and countless others during
their time spent abroad. But how do you go about having a peak
experience in Italy? I've found that the most incredible adventures
take you out of your comfort zone, lead you down unknown roads,
and involve relationships with people. Among the topics I'll cover
in this chapter is attitude, because as Galileo Galilei said, *"Diet-
ro ogni problema c'è un'opportunità"* (Behind any problem, there is
an opportunity). While I have no doubt you will encounter some
problems on your trip, they needn't derail it. If fact, they might
just enhance your experience. I'll also discuss holidays and festivals, where culture, fun, and adventure collide. Getting off the
beaten path and making local connections are related ideas and can
fill your days with meaningful, authentic encounters. Together,
these are powerful tools that you can use as the architect of your
own peak experiences.

When I think about attitude, I'm reminded of something I once
heard an acquaintance say while summarizing their trip to Italy:
"The bread is so dry. You don't even get any butter with it." It may

be a trivial example, but an attitude that focuses on the negative aspects can undoubtedly sabotage a journey that could potentially transform your life. You have the power to choose your lens. Think about whether or not something is indeed a problem. Does it impact your safety? Or is it merely something different in Italy to your own country? These travelers decided to focus on bread, ignoring the entire cultural heritage of Italy's cuisine.

You may not like everything, but try not to worry about things you can't change; focus on what you love about Italy every day. Even moments waiting in an airport line are opportunities to people-watch and appreciate Italian fashion. While stuck on a delayed train, I've had some enriching experiences, feeling camaraderie with fellow passengers, and engaging in great conversations about their lives and interests. In one instance, I recall chuckling with an Italian woman who spoke wistfully about Pop-Tarts, a breakfast she had tried in the US and now missed in Italy. Another time, I was invited to visit a newfound "train friend" in Germany, and once a fellow passenger emailed me an unpublished book manuscript. Anecdotes aside, when you perceive something as an inconvenience, channel the mindset of Roman Emperor Marcus Aurelius, who said, "You have power over your mind—not outside events. Realize this, and you will find strength." This chapter provides advice on several key elements that will enable you to make the most of your time in Italy.

Holiday and Festivals

Festivals and holidays in Italy are a key part of the culture and seeking them out is a rewarding way to learn more about the country and its people. On a visit to Florence, a crowded, some might say over-toured destination, I decided that I would book a B&B in Fiesole, a small *comune* of Florence. This picturesque hilltop town, with its Etruscan-Roman archaeological area, seemed like the ideal base. It was in a serene location, just five kilometers (3.5 miles) outside of the city, yet still easily accessible through a regular bus service. I recall the B&B owner Sara as a gracious, talkative host, whose generous breakfasts were the perfect start to every day. She told me about the Festa de l'Unità, a local festival. Just a few miles away, I knew the piazzas in Florence would be overrun with tourists and vendors peddling cheap light-up toy rockets, so I opted for the Fiesole festival, which was situated on a grassy hill overlooking Florence. Refreshingly, it was teeming with people from the neighborhood who welcomed me as one of their own. I navigated my way to a line and purchased a meal ticket. Under a tent, the locals served a variety of meats and plates of pasta they had prepared. I was overcome with emotion as I took in live theater outdoors, chatted with vendors, observed real Italian life, and even was invited to participate in an impromptu yoga class. People were friendly, curious about why I was there, and excited to speak English to a non-Italian speaker. This festival, isolated from the bustle of Florence, ended up being the highlight of my visit. I'll never forget it.

Again and again, these types of unexpected moments have consistently been the high points of my trips abroad. Festivals allow you to enjoy a fun slice of local life as they teach you about the culture, food, and people. As if at a party, spectators are in a good mood and happy to engage with visitors. Prices are lower than at events geared toward tourists, and the quality is outstanding. But beyond that, I always see something done differently in ways I wouldn't ever have thought of. It sparks curiosity into creative new ways of doing something, whether it's innovative functional design, a new approach to beauty, or a cultural practice. Italy seems to find a way to artfully merge all these ideas.

How can you have these types of experiences? In my discussion with Cassandra Santoro, the founder and CEO of Travel Italian Style (www.travelitalianstyle.com), she mentioned tapping into religious festivals. In fact, during the peak of summer tourist season in the trendy Amalfi coast region, she frequents the numerous celebrations of its patron saints. Cassandra often finds she and her friends are the only English speakers in the crowd. To find these events, she recommends you look up the patron saints of the areas where you'll stay or keep your eyes peeled for unassuming flyers often plastered around town. You can follow the seasons for activities around harvests and typical products. As locals can be a phenomenal resource, ask them what events are coming up. The *Festa del Pane* (Bread Festival) held in my ancestral village, Roio Poggio, is a fitting example of what you might experience if you dig narrowly into a town's culture. Under the azure skies and abundant sunshine of the month of August, *i roiani* (people from Roio), bedecked in colorful historical costumes, are united through dancing, singing, and processions through the streets. An army of *signore* (ladies), flashing beautiful smiles, knead gooey dough and then give life back to the community's ancient ovens, pulling from them hearty bread, which comes out in all sorts of unique shapes and creative designs. My favorite has the appearance of a child's doll, complete with braided hair. This event celebrates the central role that bread has on the table and preserves local traditions.

Up and down Italy, from its mountains and valleys to its cities and seaside towns, you will find countless festivals that evoke the same spirit as *Roio Poggio's Festa del Pane*. In truth, a volume of books could be written to chronicle the traditions around holidays in Italy, what foods are eaten, and differences among regions. But for your background knowledge, I will give you a flavor of some major holidays. This is intended to be a springboard that will enable you to seek out festivals and talk to locals to learn about their customs. In this book's supplemental material, you can find a list of major public holidays and celebrations. Not all will be listed, as many cities, communes, and regions have feast days specific to their area with their unique traditions. One commonality is that on religious feast days, masses are held that the faithful attend in addition to any local customs.

Starting with the New Year, Italians wish each other *"Buon Anno!"* (Happy New Year!) and typically welcome the future with lentils and pork, thought to symbolize wealth. Another tradition for the new year is wearing red underwear, a superstition that is said to bring good fortune. Moving a few months forward, another vital celebration is *Pasqua* (Easter), synonymous with large chocolate eggs and the *Colomba*, a dove-shaped cake. Again, regional traditions will vary, and religious Italians will attend mass to celebrate the resurrection of Christ. In Napoli, you'll find the *pastiera napoletana*, a creamy cake made with ricotta, eggs, dough, cooked grain, citrus, and other ingredients. Also, in this region, there is a festival bread called *casatiello*, filled with what an Italian might characterize as *ogni ben di Dio* (every good thing God has created), hard-boiled eggs, *pancetta*, *salame*, *provolone*, etc. Growing up, my southern Italian grandmother would fill hers with whatever was in her fridge. Italians may also eat lamb, eggs, and homemade pasta on this holy day, though this barely scratches the surface. Many will go on vacations over Easter. The following Monday is also a holiday, known as *Pasquetta*, when droves take to the countryside to enjoy picnics or local events.

Ferragosto traces its origins to Roman times when Emperor Augustus proclaimed a month to celebrate the harvest. In modern times, the Catholic Church associated it with Assumption Day, (when Jesus' mother, the Virgin Mary, ascended to heaven) which is celebrated on August 15. However, Italians refer to the entire week which includes the fifteenth of August as *Ferragosto*, when many leave the sweltering cities and take vacations. The beach is a popular option. Suppose you're traveling to Italy in August to tour cities, you may find that some businesses are closed, and local life is nearly nonexistent as tourists take over the streets.

"Natale con i tuoi, Pasqua con chi vuoi" is a well-known Italian saying. It means that Natale (Christmas) is celebrated with your family. At the same time, Pasqua can be spent with friends or whomever you like. Christmas includes religious celebrations, processions, manger scenes, and the exchange of gifts. As you know by now, Italy is highly regional, and so are the foods eaten for holidays. At Christmas in northern Italy, depending on your geography and among other dishes, you might find *agnolotti*, a small meat-filled pasta, and *bollito*, a stew of boiled meats and vegetables. You might see *lasagne*, stewed cod, or lamb in central Italy. In southern Italy,

the table may boast *spaghetti alle vongole* (with clams) or *struffoli,* a dessert made of small balls of dough in syrup. In the Campania region, many eat *capitone,* a female eel. These are only a few examples of the innumerable dishes that are part of Christmas celebrations across Italy. While Italian Americans celebrate Feast of the Seven Fishes across the Atlantic, it's not a tradition in Italy. It's possible it occurred in a small village and became popular in the United States or was simply invented in America.

Local Guides

Suppose you want to dig even deeper and ensure an authentic experience. Another suggestion Cassandra made was hiring a local guide, who, in essence, can be like a friend and take you off the beaten path. Guides in Italy must be licensed, and the process to become one is pretty rigorous, so you can expect a good return on your investment for a minimal cost. You can find a local guide with a travel planner, Googling is great for reading reviews, and increasingly, it can be helpful to find a guide on Instagram. The advantage of Instagram is that it allows you to visualize how time with the guide will be spent. You could take this idea of hiring a local a step further by hiring a family. What I mean is choosing an experience where you can live with a host family. Stefania Belli recommended this to know the culture more deeply. Her business La Lingua La Vita (www.lalingualavita.com) in Todi offers homestays for as short as one week. Enrolling in a language or culture class and pairing it with a homestay will immerse you into the culture. Airbnb promotes paired experiences with its lodging, which is another resource to connect with a cultural guide.

Stepping Off the Beaten Path

When taking college students abroad, one assignment is a mutual favorite. I identify an attractive, off-the-beaten-path village and tell my students to find their way there without technology and to put their phones away for the day. I ask them to look around, get a sense of the place, and find out what makes it tick; familiarize themselves with who the locals are, and understand what is unique to the area and its people. I ask that they engage with local people and ask them about their town and advice on what they should see, then spend hours exploring and learning about the area. The students love it because it gives them the freedom to have an unscripted adventure and not rely on a Google map or online restaurant review. The caveat is that you'll want to ensure it is not in a dangerous area. In Italy, most small villages and towns are pretty safe but do some preliminary research if you are not confident. Secondly, keep a low profile and be humble in your approach, mindful that your actions impact a local community.

A *flâneur* is a French term that refers to an urban explorer, someone who wanders the streets for pure leisure. Nineteenth-century Parisian writer Charles Baudelaire described this as being, "…away from home and yet to feel oneself everywhere at home; to see the world, to be at the center of the world, and yet to remain hidden from the world—impartial natures which the tongue can but clumsily define. The spectator is a prince who everywhere rejoices in his incognito. The lover of life makes the whole world his family…"[3] This idea has been backed up by modern-day science with a study in "Real-World Exploration" published in *Psychological Science* in 2022, which found that novel experiences and exploration through random wandering are connected to increased happiness and social connectivity.

Many of my favorite experiences in Italy are always utterly random. I once happened upon a university graduation and observed the tradition of students wearing laurel wreaths upon their heads. Another time, after I saw a flyer for a community theater performance in Florence, I purchased a ticket and laughed aloud as I enjoyed the show and connected with local residents, sharing

---

[3] Charles Baudelaire, *The Painter of Modern Life and Other Essays*, trans. Jonathan Mayne (London: Phaidon, 1964), 43.

a moment in real Florentine life. Even if you are staying in a large tourist hub, find a day to get away to a smaller town or even a more residential neighborhood and unassumingly become part of a local landscape. While you're at it, wander the streets, going from one tiny shop to the next, assembling a meal to savor in a park or peaceful corner of a piazza (so long as it's permitted by the town).

If you use your senses, you will discover scores of intriguing moments. I'll never forget seeing two laborers eating fresh mozzarella and prosciutto in their work truck while sharing a mini bottle of wine. Wander down a side street at the right moment, and you'll hear the melodic sound of dishes and pick up the irresistible aroma of Italian home cooking wafting from the window as the afternoon news plays in the background. Unscripted local moments can be culturally insightful, downright magical, and often are the hidden gems, such as a restaurant I discovered en route to Sestri Levante (a potential base destination for those wishing to visit the Cinque Terre).

Driving the autostrada, my family's stomachs grumbled. In a valley of wooded and hilly terrain, we spotted a quaint village dominated by an ornate church spire and separated from the highway by a shallow stream. Full of hope that there might be somewhere to eat, we rolled the dice and took the exit. Stepping out of the car and into Trattoria al Vecchio Scalo in the little hamlet of Isola del Cantone, I scanned the restaurant's eclectic décor. It was enveloped by wood paneling and immediately overwhelmed us: walls festooned with dusty liquor bottles, old sports trophies, dozens of ornamental plates adorning the pale-yellow walls, along with kitschy knickknacks and old photographs. While nearly deserted, the aromas drifting from the back were reminiscent of my Italian grandmother's kitchen—jackpot. I recall sitting with my family, enjoying the daily specials in a warm environment that felt like being in a relative's basement for a meal. We chatted with our waiter, Walter, a man in his sixties whose face was framed by square glasses and a salt-and-pepper beard. Curious about each other, we learned that he was a retired businessman who had spent time in the US and discussed why we ended up in his village. As we were leaving, we had the privilege of meeting Walter's grandchildren on their way back from school to have lunch at the family restaurant. I smile every time I think about this simple roadside stop.

Now, I'll contrast this with a group of students I saw on the terrace of what I'll call a tourist trap restaurant opposite the Pantheon in Rome. The area was teeming with visitors snapping selfies, vendors hawking souvenirs, a cacophony of loudly spoken English, and aggressive waiters beckoning passersby to eat there as they touted free shots of limoncello and flirted with female patrons. Of course, all of this was set to the melodic tones of *The Godfather* theme song playing in the background. While everyone has their own idea of a meaningful experience, this scene makes me cringe as it's more akin to a twisted artificial Italian theme park. Authenticity is one of the most essential elements of a meaningful trip to Italy. It can be simple, but you'll need to step away from the hotspots, even a few blocks, to find it. One of the goals of this book is to help you move away from staged authenticity and become immersed in real life.

Unscripted experiences can make for an adventurous day. Nonetheless, it can be helpful to learn a little about your destination before leaving for Italy. Questions to consider are what is the history of the area? Which foods are specialties? What are the key industries? Look into the local events, leisure activities, art, and culture. An excellent place to start is Italy's official tourist website (www.italia.it/en). If you want to connect with a local area, look no further than the *Borghi Più Belli d'Italia*. This group promotes villages in Italy known for their beauty and exceptional cultural heritage. Searching the webpage, for example, just an hour and a half from Rome's chaos, you'll find an experience called *"Castel di Tora, natura e sport insieme agli asinelli"* on Lake Turano. According to the description on the Borghi Più Belli d'Italia's website (borghipiubelliditalia.it), you'll be surrounded by spectacular pastures, enjoy a boat ride, and even go on a hiking excursion where you'll be accompanied by two donkeys, all while staying in a picturesque bed and breakfast.

Another approach is to explore Slow Cities or *Cittaslow* in Italian, an idea that can be traced back to the Slow Food movement and spreads the basic concepts beyond just food to health and authentic living. It's about "curious people of a recovered time, where man is still the protagonist of the slow and healthy succession of seasons, respectful of citizens' health, the authenticity of products and good food, rich of fascinating craft traditions of valuable works of art, squares, theaters, shops, cafés, restaurants, places of the spirit and unspoiled landscapes, characterized by the spontaneity of religious rites, respect of traditions through the joy of a slow and quiet living," says the Slow Food Organization's website (www.cittaslow.org). Here, also, a list of these towns can be found. In the Slow City of Chiavenna, a local guide escorted me around, which is an ideal way to delve into the history and local culture. In Chiavenna, you could learn about local specialties like *bresaola* (cured beef) or *pizzoccheri*, buckwheat pasta of Valtellina, traditionally made with scraps of cheese and abundant butter, as well as tour *crotti* or small caves, which are still used to store foods like cheeses. Even though they are made of stone, their unique airflow keeps everything fresh and cool. Rich experiences in small communities are fodder for great stories and learning.

You may want to consider staying in a smaller, less visited location as your base. Choosing a farm stay, known as an *agriturismo*, is one way to approach this (see chapter VI, Casa Dolce Casa). Traveling by car can be helpful in reaching off the beaten path destinations, but it's not a prerequisite to enjoying small town life and authentic Italy. Countless locations are easily reachable by train and bus, and even large, tourist-populated cities have their share of hidden local sites for you to discover.

Cultural Mindfulness

Recently, I saw a review for a restaurant I had eaten at in Rome. It read: "Refused us service – had been for dinner elsewhere and wanted to stop somewhere close to the hotel for a drink and maybe something sweet. Was around 10 pm and had quite a few empty tables, asked if we could grab one of the outside tables to have a drink and was point blank refused. Was told to 'go to a bar'. Quite rude really being as we wanted a drink and something off the dessert menu. No explanation, just sent on our way. Not friendly and wouldn't recommend!" The restaurant posted the following response, "Good evening, you asked for a coffee, but we are a restaurant not a bar and we have shown you the bar 20 meters from us with the tables outside."

While a trivial example, it points to the notion of cultural mindfulness. I characterize this as being sensitive to cultural issues. Reflection, knowing yourself and personal or cultural biases, can help approach cultural humility. A simple way to think of this is don't assume that the same rules apply abroad, and when they don't, accept it. Use it as an opportunity to reflect on the differences in your culture. Is it something that matters, or is it the frustration of being caught off guard when an experience doesn't match ethnocentric expectations? Think of these as our cultural standards. It's also about considering the perspectives of others and being cognizant, not merely using your culture as the yardstick; realize that there are reasons people have certain behaviors, and it may be cultural instead of personal. As a metaphor, it doesn't make sense to play a baseball game following soccer rules. Think about an Italian coming to a coffee shop in the US and writing a bad review because they were served their drink in a paper cup, an accepted practice in the US but unexpected in Italy. Being patient in new situations will go a long way.

The disgruntled person who wrote the above restaurant review likely looked at the issue from their perspective. Did they consider that Italian restaurants don't operate the same way as what they were used to? Was there any thought that it might be abnormal in Italy to go to a trattoria for after-dinner drinks? Did it cross their mind that the workforce of Italy's mostly family-owned *trattorie* may have limited staffing and might not have the capacity to serve as a bar? On the flip side, this trattoria may have felt that they were doing the tourists a favor by providing directions on where they could go for a drink.

Ida Castiglioni mentioned that many travelers should know that they have their own cultures. This is an excellent reminder to step back and reflect on the customs, traditions, and accepted practices in your country that might not make sense to someone else. Just because you are used to certain cultural norms does not mean it's the universal way to approach the situation. At the same time, be mindful that people will automatically make assumptions about you depending on where you come from.

Another idea to consider in terms of cultural humility is that tourism often displays the most enjoyable aspects of local life. We can miss a lot below the surface. Visitors might need to be made aware of the daily grind for locals. They rightfully compliment the Italians they meet on how lucky they are to live in Italy, pointing out aspects of its beauty and how wonderful the food tastes. A tourist, however, doesn't have to endure the day-to-day challenges that an Italian might lament, such as high taxes, expensive goods, limited opportunities to earn money, high unemployment, a vast bureaucracy, issues with public corruption, and disorganization. In fact, by 2021, Italy had forty-four prime ministers since the founding of the Italian Republic in 1946, and some cities have systemic issues that cause huge mounds of trash to pile up on the streets.

Tourists who only seem to know about caricatures of Italian food and Hollywood mob movies might come across as impolite. Those with Italian origins may bring up an Italian-American (-Australian, -Canadian, etc.) tradition that one of their ancestors brought with them from their village, discounting the regionality of Italy. It can be fun to have conversations about your identity and customs, but you may be surprised at Italians' reactions. Realize that many of these exported traditions were regional or isolated to a village and were unknown in most of Italy. Even practices common in Italy a century ago evolved in different directions or disappeared over the years. And they were influenced by the melting pot of their ancestor's adopted country.

If you do have Italian origins, be proud of them. How you describe your connection matters in terms of how it is understood. In Italy, saying you're Italian-American, for example, implies that you have dual citizenship or were born in Italy. To avoid confusion and demonstrate respect, it is best to say, "My origins are Italian," "My grandmother was from..." etc., rather than "I'm Italian." A helpful phrase may be *"Sono di origine italiana"* (My origins are Italian). Those with dual citizenship but little knowledge about contemporary culture in Italy might be better received if they simply say, *"Ho doppia cittadinanza"* (I have dual citizenship) when discussing this topic. However, in most cases, there is little benefit in mentioning you have dual citizenship and no reason to advertise that you carry multiple passports.

Connecting Meaningfully with Locals

The good life is built with good relationships.
—DR. ROBERT J. WALDINGER

In fact, research demonstrates that people who live the happiest, healthiest lives are those who have strong social connections. My best days in Italy are always when I have a meaningful, fun, inspirational, or unexpected interaction with someone I meet. Italians are incredibly social and relationship-orientated, which may help explain why they have among the highest life expectancy worldwide. Most Italians are inherently friendly and will want to connect with you, so take the leap and connect with them. One piece of advice on connecting with others came from a diplomat I had invited to speak to a group I was working with. During his career in posts abroad, he said that you can look through the human lens when in doubt. We all share humanity and have hopes and dreams. We want our children or families to have a better future. Then, he quipped, we all have a mother-in-law. Connecting on common hopes, joys, and struggles can be a powerful way to spark a relationship.

During one trip to Italy, my then six-year-old son and I started visiting a little *pasticceria* and *bar* (pastry shop and bar) for breakfast. He would get a little bottle of peach juice and a croissant, and I'd order a cappuccino. After the third day, he was greeted heartily by name and *"Buongiorno! Come stai? Succo di pesca e una brioche, giusto?"* (Good morning! How are you? A peach juice and a croissant, right?" My boy would sheepishly grin and say, *"Sto bene. Sì, grazie."* (I'm well. Yes, thank you.) This made us feel like part of the community, even after a few days.

If you're visiting Italy for a week or two, I advise against moving locations every few days. There are benefits to limiting your engagement with one or two areas. Focusing on one place, you will experience local culture, build relationships, and see more of the region. It takes time to learn to navigate a new location, know the transportation system, and understand what it offers. Traveling to another far-away destination consumes time, can be tiring, and you'll have the inconvenience of transporting luggage. With that said, I do advocate for regional mobility. Taking day trips is an excellent option if you're in one area; you'll discover new places in the context of your home base and can do this with a smaller bag. Trying to see too much and check things off a bucket list might make for great Instagram posts, but you'll likely only scratch the surface of the destination by visiting major tourist attractions and miss the authentic culture of a place.

I asked Cassandra Santoro her thoughts on how to connect with locals. She said there are certain things that locals get asked all the time. There's a difference between inquiring about a local cultural event rather than what's their favorite restaurant. Find a genuine reason to connect. In your approach with locals, reflect on what you can offer them, not just take from them. For example, taking a picture of a local can sometimes be using them as a human souvenir. Instead, researching the local area's culture and asking locals to tell you their story allows them to be heard. It goes a long way in learning from each other and making a real connection. In that spirit, Cassandra started making videos where she gives locals space to share their backgrounds and perspectives. This is great advice, and I would take this a step further. When you engage with locals, attempt to do it in their language. In fact, I've seen firsthand how knowledge of Italian can arguably be the best tool you have in your toolkit that enables you to have peak experiences in Italy—you will be much more likely to make friends and gain an insider's perspective. This starts with even a few simple words. When you begin to see the doors that open, my guess is that you will want to learn even more. The next chapter will explore this topic further and give you strategies that enhance your ability to absorb Italian.

V

Learning Italian

To have another language is to possess a second soul.
— CHARLEMAGNE

One of the most impactful ways to embody *la bella figura* (make a good impression, see Chapter III) and enjoy a peak experience (see Chapter IV) is to learn a few courtesy phrases in Italian. Because of this I feel that having this basic language ability is an essential requirement for anyone visiting Italy. For short-term travelers, if you can extend that to a handful or so important vocabulary words and phrases, and understand how pronunciation works, it will give you confidence, open doors, and connect you to locals. If you are planning to stay more than a few weeks, a baseline knowledge of Italian is a must. Throughout this book and in the appendix, I've included carefully selected words and phrases that I've found particularly useful. While this is a great foundation, I'll also give you some strategies and tips to accelerate your learning.

In my many years teaching Italian to adult learners and college students, I've often heard comments like, "I'm just no good at languages" or, "Don't you need a special aptitude to learn a language?" Let me tell you, my experience teaching thousands of adult learners and college students has taught me that anyone, including those of you with doubts, can make impressive progress and even become conversant in a second language. While fluency is a laudable goal, it isn't necessary to have a truly enriching experience communicating. All you need to do is lay the groundwork to make connections.

Motivation

We all need a reason to tackle something new, especially if it's daunting. Dig deep and vividly envision the experiences you'll have and friends you'll make. Imagine sipping a cappuccino at the counter of a cozy Italian *bar*. As you bite into a crisp croissant (or *cornetto* in Italian), buttery flakes float down like snowflakes onto the counter. There's a buzz of people. You smile and exchange a few words in Italian with fellow patrons and the barista about your trip. Before you know it, you are getting flooded with great advice and insider tips about your destination. Remember that everything you learn is like a small key that unlocks a new opportunity. Maintain a positive attitude and celebrate the progress you make. Even if it's just one new word, you will be amazed at where it takes you.

Make Engaging with the Culture a Habit

If you plan to spend significant time in Italy, or committing more deeply to learning Italian is a goal, I'll suggest a few strategies. Watch films, listen to music, and learn about the food as much as possible. Incorporate Italian into your everyday life. Many Netflix shows allow you to change the audio and subtitles into Italian. One idea is to watch something you know well in Italian to get the feel of it and improve your skills. You might also view an Italian film once a week. By doing so, you'll learn about the culture and language simultaneously. RadioItalia is a radio station that only plays Italian music, and they have a great free app for your phone; even the commercials allow you to practice listening skills and pick up cultural nuggets.

The trick is to add Italian to what you already do. When washing dishes, taking a walk, or driving to work, play a podcast or listen to music. Is it time to relax? Then, check out an Italian film. At least one month before departure, set a goal of how much time you can fit in to absorb Italian each week. At a minimum, I'd say make it a few hours. If this commitment seems daunting, what I'll call "learning snacks," count. You can try ten minutes on

Duolingo before bed each day, twenty minutes listening to Italian while straightening the house, thirty minutes looking over a few verbs and one Netflix show with Italian subtitles. Keep it fun and exciting whenever possible and make it a habit. Keep tabs and add up how much time you spend toward your weekly goal. Chances are two hours each week will be easy.

You can review what you have learned anytime. As you go through your routine, ask yourself how you'd say what you're doing in Italian. Are you ordering a coffee? Think, "How would I do this in Italy? What would I say? How would this experience be different?" If you aren't sure how to say a word, I encourage you to use Word Reference. It comes as a free app, and unlike Google Translate, it provides context behind words and colloquialisms. Context is vital as some words you'd look up from English to Italian could be mistranslated. Think about bark. A dog barks, but trees have bark. In case you were wondering, *abbaia* is the Italian verb bark. Instead of woof, Italians describe the sound dogs make as *bau*.

Keep a journal or make notes on your phone or a device like an iPad or computer. You can write down new words and expressions and how much time you spent learning in different categories there. When you reach your goal each week, reward yourself with a cappuccino, a bottle of wine, or something else that excites you for your Italian adventure.

Gestures

Not long ago, I was watching an inspirational piece about a woman mountain climber on Rai, Italy's public television station. After losing one of her hands, she courageously took up climbing to show the world she could overcome challenges. While the story was compelling, it was fascinating to see her gesticulate with the arm that was missing a hand. To me, it demonstrated just how ingrained gestures are in the culture; they are passed from parents to children, along with the spoken language. The roots are deep. Going back to Roman times, gestures were literally a matter of life and death. When gladiators fought, thumbs up meant let him live, and thumbs down meant death. While they exist in English (think about a child crossing their fingers as they swear something to be true), it's hard to witness an Italian conversation without gestures. Sometimes Italians are merely moving their hands, but often gestures have distinct meanings. *Speak Italian, The Fine Art of the Gesture* provides a great illustrated resource. However, the internet also abounds with videos and examples. I advise observing them and not copying something unless you know what it means, which may vary across regions. Be very careful not to appropriate any obscene gesture. Even in jest, you could offend someone or appear to be mocking the culture. For example, holding up your index finger and pinky while grasping your middle fingers with your thumb to make horns is known as *corna* and can imply someone's spouse is cheating on them. Some hand symbols are innocuous or for emphasis, such as only holding up one's pinky finger to indicate that someone is rail thin. Another is to put your palms together as if in prayer to ask for a favor. Or placing your index finger on your cheek indicates something is delicious. The origin of gestures isn't entirely known. It could be related to ancient Roman and Greek cultures and the multitude of mutually unintelligible languages that its occupants spoke across Italy's history.

A Quick Guide to Italian Pronunciation

In minutes, you can learn to pronounce just about any Italian word reasonably well and intelligibly. You should rely on the many Italian terms incorporated into English vocabulary to help you understand the basics more quickly. Note that this guide is intentionally simplified, but it's still a good baseline to build off.

ANCHOR PRONUNCIATION TO WHAT YOU ALREADY KNOW

For speakers of English, Italian pronunciation is embedded into many English words. Italian is also phonetic, meaning it's pronounced as spelled, so once you know the rules, you can pronounce just about anything. As a result of years of foreign influence, invasions, and a fragmented state, regional dialects exist. However, in modern-day Italy, nearly everyone understands Italian, the official language of the government. The accent will vary in different regions, but you may not pick up on it unless you have advanced abilities.

Cooking, music, and the arts are great examples of Italian words already in your vocabulary. Using these words as a reference point will make learning the sound patterns much more straightforward. For instance, it might not be obvious how to pronounce "ci" instead of "chi." But when I put them in front of two words you already know, the greeting *ciao* and the food *gnocchi*, it's natural. By the way, the "gn" is not said as "no", it's pronounced as the "ny" sound in "canyon." *Ballerina* and *barista* provide insight into Italian's phonetic nature, meaning all the letters and vowels are pronounced. This is much simpler than English, with its many silent letter and vowel combinations. Despite not being authentically Italian, Starbucks has done a big favor to those wanting to learn Italian. Many drink names like *venti* and *grande* can teach you Italian pronunciation. *Caffè macchiato* reminds us that "chi" is a "k" or hard sound, and that downward sloping accent (known as the grave accent) signifies a closed-off sound, meaning we stop it short or draw it back toward us, whereas the acute accent slopes up and is an open sound. Think of going to your favorite café. The sound projects away from you as you speak. While this level of nuance is nice to know, it's not essential for you to start communicating. Look at the following examples and see if you can identify the patterns. Initially, words like these are beneficial in guiding your pronunciation until it becomes second nature.

Ballerina	Gnocchi	Grande
Barista	Latte	Spaghetti
Ciao	Cappuccino	Panino
Chianti	Venti	

ITALIAN VOWELS

A – ah, as in fAther
Italian examples: villa, lava, mafia, trattoria
E (closed) – ay, as in bAy
Italian examples: latte, finale
E (open) – eh, as in bEd
Italian examples: al fresco, tempo, cello, tortellini
I – E, as in feet
Italian examples: ravioli, tutti frutti
O (closed) – oh, as in bOat
Italian examples: piccolo, bravo, risotto
O (open) – aw, as in bOUght
Italian example: opera
U – ew, as in bOOt
Italian examples: cappuccino, tutti frutti, Bruno

ITALIAN CONSONANTS

Most are similar to the English pronunciation. However, pay particular attention to the below letters and combinations.

C – ca/co/cu
Hard C sound (like English "k")
Italian examples: cannoli, terracotta
C – chi/che
Hard C sound (like English "k")
Italian examples: gnocchi, chianti, orchestra, macchiato, Pinocchio
C – ci/ce
Soft C sound (like English "ch" in "church")
Italian examples: cello, cappuccino
G – ga/go/gu
Hard G sound (like English "g" in "go")
Italian examples: regata, gondola
G – ghe/ghi

Hard G sound (like English "g" in "go")
Italian examples: spaghetti, pizza margherita
G – gi/ge
Soft G sound (like English "j" in "jet")
Italian examples: gelato, Gina
Gli – "ye" as in "ye olde days of yore"
Italian example: tagliatelle
Gn – "gn" as in lasagna
Italian example: gnocchi
H – at the beginning of the word, h is silent. H only functions to make a "g" or "c" into a hard sound before an "i" or "e."
Italian examples: hotel ("otel"), ciao vs. chianti, ghetto vs. gelato
R – trilled or rolled, as it is in Spanish. If you can't make this sound, just pronounce it as an "r"

ACCENTS

Typically, the penultimate (second to last) syllable is emphasized. There are many exceptions, which will be learned as you increase your exposure to Italian. Some examples are zu-CCHI-ni, mi-ne-STRO-ne. When the last syllable is accented, it is stressed, as in caffè.

Learn Some Key Verbs

There are several irregular verbs that are worth memorizing. If you don't have time, I'd recommend you learn the first-person conjugation (I form) for a few important ones. Imagine how many times you will want to communicate *vado* (I go), *voglio* (I want), or *ho* (I have), for example. With a quick internet search, you find multitudes of resources to find these conjugations easily online.

Volere	to want
Dovere	to have to

Potere	to be able to
Fare	to do or to make
Stare	to be feeling (good or bad)
Dare	to give
Essere	to be
Avere	to have
Andare	to go
Uscire	to go out

Outside of some of the irregular verbs listed above, Italian conjugations are relatively straightforward: verbs end in *-are, -ere,* and *-ire.* It shouldn't take a significant investment to learn the basics. Verbs ending with *-are* are the simplest. In most cases, you drop the *-are* and add the correct vowel (see the Appendix). If you want to talk about yourself, add an "o" once the ending is dropped. Since this is not an Italian grammar book, I won't go into depth. However, learn a few patterns, and you'll exponentially enhance your communication abilities. Even if you only learn the present tense, you can always add *domani* (tomorrow) or *ieri* (yesterday) to the sentence. While not technically grammatically correct in using the present tense, it will get the point across. Of course, if you have time, try to learn the past tense and grammatical nuances.

Potere (to be able to), *dovere* (to have to), and *volere* (to want) are called modal verbs. This means that if you conjugate them and follow with any verb in the infinitive (the unconjugated form of the verb), you can communicate loads of information. *Posso* (I can), followed by *mangiare* (to eat), gives you "I can eat." *Voglio* followed by *parlare* (to speak), means "I want to speak." *Devo* (I have to) followed by *andare* (to go) is translated to "I have to go." Once you know a few verbs and this pattern, you'll be amazed at what you can say. To make a sentence negative, you can put *non* before the verb. *"Non voglio mangiare"* would be "I do not want to eat."

The Italian way of talking about likes and dislikes is similar in using an unconjugated verb. Use *mi piace* (literally "it is pleasing to me" but translated to "I like") to say *"Mi piace mangiare"* (I like to eat), for example. You can also use *Mi piace* to discuss nouns you like. *"Mi piace la pasta"* (I like the pasta). If the noun you like is plural, you'd say *Mi piacciono* instead of *Mi piace*. For example, *"Mi piacciono le scarpe"* (I like the shoes). To reverse it and indicate you do not like something, all you have to do is put *non* in front of the sentence. So to express that you don't like the pasta, you'd say *"Non mi piace la pasta"* (I don't like the pasta).

Learn About What You Love

Memorizing articles, gender, and grammatical structures is a sure-fire way to turn most people off of learning a language. Instead, learn about your interests in Italian. Learning a language is about communicating, not perfection. Once you know a few basics, learn words that match your interests. Whether golf, hiking, history, painting, cooking, sports, or something else, you can search for clips on YouTube, Instagram, Facebook, or TikTok in Italian. This will motivate you and make learning the vocabulary more effortless. What's better is that you'll likely absorb cultural differences and other words around the context. From there, everything will build. When you travel to Italy, you will be in a better spot to engage with locals about topics that interest you. You can take this further by pursuing some of your hobbies while abroad. Even if you take a formal course or use a language learning app, you should supplement your studies with what you love.

When Not to Use Italian

I speak Spanish to God, Italian to women, French to men,
and German to my horse.
—HOLY ROMAN EMPEROR CHARLES V

Although this is an amusing quote, it makes the point that there is appropriate language for every circumstance. I'll suggest we add, "I use English when I'm in trouble" to this quote. As an undergraduate student, I purchased a Eurorail pass that was valid for five trips. On my first train ride, I assumed that when they came around to check tickets, they would validate mine and explain how I use it. When the Trenitalia employee made his rounds, I handed it to him. He took one look and said in Italian, "This hasn't been validated." Thinking I could talk my way out of the situation, I explained in Italian that I had misunderstood. The ticket control officer replied that I had to travel without a ticket. Then, he walked away with my ticket and continued to check on other passengers. I was stunned. Not sure what to do, I followed him around. I went into a long explanation in English about how I didn't understand what was happening and lobbied for the return of my ticket. Magically, something switched. He validated it for me and explained how to use it. I recounted this to my Italian cousins, who laughed and said, "Yes, this always works." When in a jam or dealing with authorities, you may make things worse if you try to take on the situation in Italian.

VI

Casa Dolce Casa

*Chi si volta, e chi si gira, sempre a casa va finire.
(No matter where you go or turn, you
will always end up at home.)*
—ITALIAN PROVERB

Location Isn't Everything

Your choice of where to stay in terms of location and type of accommodation can be a factor in the kind of experiences you will have. There is no shortage of options in Italy, and they are incredibly diverse. I'll cover the major ones—hotels, hostels, apartments, B&Bs, and farm stays—where I expect the majority of travelers will stay. However, if you are looking for something different, know that there are unique possibilities such as camping, convents and monasteries, and even mountain huts, where you can rest your head. When I travel to Italy for brief periods, I typically seek out a bed and breakfast (not necessarily on Airbnb or Vrbo), reading the ratings carefully. I look for the highest rated and then read the reviews to determine what will be the best fit. I like B&Bs because they provide an opportunity for a connection with the locals who run them and get me away from more crowded, sometimes impersonal hotels. I also think that apartments are a great choice if you plan to stay in one location more than a few days. You may have access to more space, a washing machine, and a kitchen. These amenities may allow you to save money while increasing your level of comfort and offering you a true Italian experience. Nonetheless, hotels can be a convenient option for short term travelers, especially in larger cities.

In choosing the location of where you'll stay overnight, it can be useful to understand the layout of cities and towns in Italy, which have some similarities across the board. In the historic center, you will find many buildings significant to the cultural heritage, as well as cathedrals and churches, shopping, and restaurants. The center is typically a higher-priced area for lodging, shops, and eateries. Broadly speaking, towns grew out from the center in concentric circles. The town's nucleus was often surrounded by a wall for protection from invaders. Across Italy, you will still see portions of walls, or sometimes they are nearly entirely preserved; such is the case for the seventeenth century walls in Lucca, in Tuscany. Of course, there had to be a way in and out of the city, so you will see enormous arches that once were city gates called *porte* (or *porta* in the singular form). Larger towns may designate neighborhoods by the name of the *porta*. In Milan, one of my apartments was in the Porta Romana district, just outside of where the walls had been. Interestingly, my street was called *Strada della Carità*, meaning Charity Street. The building was a several hundred-year-old converted convent, with a courtyard and remains of a historic well in the center. Apparently, it took on this name because the nuns who lived there would provide those unable to enter the city gates with a place to stay. The further you move out from the center, the concentration of historically significant buildings tends to diminish, and often all types of lodging will be cheaper. The railway stations are typically within walking distance of the center, in less desirable areas that can be somewhat seedy.

Lodging Options

Staying in an *albergo* (also called a *hotel* in Italian) is not entirely straightforward. There are large American-style chains in bigger cities and near airports, luxury options, boutique and family run hotels, as well as inexpensive *pensioni*. While there is a star rating, it may not be accurate and quality can be inconsistent across different hotels. Websites can be helpful, but you'll often find the best clues into a potential hotel by reviewing the travel ratings or visiting an online forum or Facebook group. Note that you are charged per person and not per room, and every guest must show an official government issued document (usually your passport) to access a room. In addition, in many cities, all types of lodging charge overnight guests a daily tax, which may be required to be paid separately in cash (*tassa di soggiorno*).

One of the biggest differences in an Italian hotel as compared to what you would find in the US is the size of the room, which tends to be significantly smaller in Italy. Another difference is the efforts to conserve electricity. In some Italian hotels, your lights or air conditioning unit (should you have one) will not turn on until you enter the room and insert your key card into a slot by the door. Hotel room keys and even key cards in some cases, are often left at the front desk when you leave the building. Usually, hotels will offer breakfast, and some will have a bar or restaurant. Amenities like a fitness center and swimming are not always common. A *pensione* is a low-budget hotel with even fewer amenities and smaller rooms, with the potential of a shared bathroom.

Youth hostels (*ostello* in Italian) are popular with younger travelers as they can be one of the most affordable lodging options. Locations can vary, but due to cost constraints, they may be outside the city center. It's not uncommon to find a dormitory-style setup with bunk beds in shared rooms, including shared bathrooms, for travelers. Some hostels offer private rooms at an additional cost.

Apartments can be rented on a variety of websites, but I recommend that you either use a well-known site like Airbnb or a travel agent who you trust. Searching the internet to find an accommodation in Italy can turn up scores of sites that ask you to wire money or put down a credit card deposit. You should approach this very cautiously and cross-reference the business before you transfer any funds. You should also read the cancellation policy. Some apartment rentals are non-refundable even months in advance. In the below section, La Casa (The Home), I'll discuss some of the features you can expect in an Italian apartment.

The notion of an *agriturismo* is a fairly recent phenomenon in Italy that has grown in popularity over the last few decades. It is a farm stay, but you can think of it as a bed and breakfast in a rural setting, often in idyllic locations with sprawling, bucolic landscapes, and seaside or mountain views. There will be some type of agricultural production, and it may include a restaurant or farm store featuring jams, cheeses, meats, or other products made onsite. Activity offerings could include horseback riding, gardening classes, or guided excursions. One of my favorite *agriturismo* experiences was in Tuscany's spectacular Val d'Orcia, a region protected as a World Heritage Site by UNESCO, and known for its cypress tree-lined roads, medieval hill towns, vineyards, golden fields, and olive groves. I stayed at a rustic farmhouse constructed of a mix of ancient rose-hued bricks and stone. It was just a ten-minute walk to the hamlet of Castiglione d'Orcia, where I recall savoring a plate of sauteed zucchini flowers stuffed with fresh ricotta. In the mornings, the owners served up homemade bread, jams, coffee, and cakes al fresco at a rustic wooden table, where swallows darted in and out of their nests in the rafters above. By car, the *agriturismo* was accessible to the surrounding hill towns and some small cities, like Siena.

B&Bs can vary greatly across Italy and can be found in cities and villages alike. Once I stayed at a B&B located in a quaint home in Cortona, the town that got some notoriety for the book *Under the Tuscan Sun*. On another trip, my B&B was a room in an apartment building right in the center of Rome where there was a basket of snacks set out in the morning and a voucher for a coffee at the Irish pub nearby. Because of the inconsistency, it's best to do some research before making your selection.

La Casa (The Home)

When I was a kid, my aunt Milena from L'Aquila, Italy, visited my family in the United States. She was terrified the entire time she was in our suburban home, which sat on an unfenced private wooded lot. Why? Even though we lived in a safe and low-crime area, she feared bandits would break into the house. Aunt Milena wasn't paranoid. An unsecured home would be out of the ordinary and likely feel uncomfortable for many Italians.

While you may stay in a hotel, with easily accessible short-term apartment and home rentals thanks to Airbnb, Vrbo, and Booking.com, to name a few, more and more visitors to Italy are renting actual homes. Because of this, it can be useful to understand a bit about what it's like in an Italian home. This information will also provide a further glimpse into the culture, and for long-term visitors, it is a must. In Italy, *una villa*, a stand-alone house, often seems like a fortress. It can be surrounded by a high wall or fence. Outside the gate is a *citofono* (intercom) that sometimes has a camera. This is also the case with many apartment buildings. The front entrance of a home can seem like a massive bank vault door that you'll need to crank several times with a long key, which has the appearance of something you might imagine a jailer in the old American west used. While this excessive security may raise your suspicions, Italy is relatively safe. I view these precautions positively. As discussed throughout this book, violent crime is infrequent, but petty crime can be a problem. Never leave your front door or windows open, or you might be a victim of theft. Refer to Chapter XI, Safety, for an in-depth discussion on this topic.

Upon entering an Italian home, you'll notice tiled or parquet floors, including in the bedrooms. Wall-to-wall carpeting, known as *la moquette*, is not considered hygienic. Typically, it's only found in hotels. Italians rarely traipse around barefoot, or in socks for that matter. While in some cultures it's polite to remove your shoes when entering someone's home as a guest, Italians simply keep theirs on. However, when relaxing in their own homes, they will remove their shoes and slip on *ciabatte*, Italian house slippers.

Using the United States for comparison, apartments in Italy will likely be a more manageable size. Operating in a smaller space comes naturally to Italians. Italy's an urbanely concentrated country of approximately sixty million that occupies a geographical territory about 30 percent smaller than the state of California—or half the size of France. Because Italian cities are ancient, many dwellings are in older, even medieval, buildings that can't be significantly altered. Thus, you may have to walk up multiple flights of stairs. In some cases, there may be tiny, painfully slow elevators that have an internal door cage that must be manually shut before it will move. Note that you need to close this upon exiting, or it won't work for the next rider who requests it.

For comparison, let's look at some general differences between homes in the United States and Italy. An Italian kitchen's proportions will be smaller. For cooking, it's common to find a gas stove, which sometimes may have to be lit by hand. Italians creatively use space, including the cooktop. Sometimes they come with a hinged board attached to the stove that folds down onto the cooktop to double as a food prep surface. The cabinet above the sink might house a built-in dishrack to merge dish storage and drying. Don't expect a dishwasher or garbage disposal, as they are scarce. In general, there are fewer appliances compared to the US. Microwaves are still uncommon in Italian homes, and refrigerators likely may have less storage capacity than you are used to. Upon visiting the US, one Italian commented that the fridges he saw were almost as big as cathedral doors.

The bathrooms are more petite, and shower stalls may be awkward for larger individuals and tend to splash water onto the bathroom floor. As a student, my first apartment in Milan only had a bathtub and a hose, where my three roommates and I had no choice but to crouch down to wash. Water pressure may seem weaker, and smaller hot water tanks could fizzle out fairly quickly. Another surprise to some visitors is the presence of the bidet, which looks like a sink on the floor and is used primarily for what you might call intimate personal hygiene.

In Italian homes, the washing machine will almost always be either in the kitchen or bathroom, not in a designated laundry room. Its controls can be an extremely complicated wheel with a dozen hieroglyphic-looking symbols. They are designed to conserve energy and operate very slowly, often taking an hour or more to complete a cycle. Regarding energy, it can be costly. Italy imports a portion of its gas from Russia, although less since the Ukraine war, and a large amount of electricity from France. Older buildings may be poorly insulated and not necessarily energy efficient. It's respectful to close doors and shut off lights when leaving a room. When leaving an apartment, house, or hotel room, shut off appliances, including air conditioning. Italians tend to conserve resources, and energy-consuming devices such as air conditioners and clothes dryers may not always be available. Clothes are often dried on drying racks, clotheslines, or above bathtubs. One of the more curious systems I experienced was a series of pullies that would raise and lower drying rods above the bathroom in an apartment I rented. Expect that you may need to hang dry your clothes all year round. In colder months, you'll learn to plan for a delay. You can also leave your clothes by the radiator to expedite drying.

Keep in mind these are generalities. Accommodations run the spectrum. Luxury homes can be stately and stunning. However, if you're traveling on a budget, be aware that living arrangements may differ from what they are accustomed to. Rather than seeking an Airbnb with a dryer, a huge kitchen, and four bedrooms, consider staying in a more traditional Italian home. It can be an opportunity to learn how to use space well, gain insight into the lifestyle, and conserve natural resources. For families, being in a more confined space might also encourage bonding.

VII

In Viaggio (Traveling)

To travel by train is to see nature and human beings, towns
and churches and rivers, in fact, to see life.
—AGATHA CHRISTIE

When traveling throughout Italy, the first image that comes to mind for many visitors is the quintessential, even romantic, notion of riding the Italian rails. If you're traversing longer distances from one major city center to another, train travel is often a great way to move around, but don't assume it's the only option. In this chapter, I'd like you to expand your thinking and cover many of the options available for travel. For example, in my experience, coach buses (private companies, not to be confused with local buses that solely travel around cities) can be a wonderful alternative to travel long distances. Fewer passengers are on board, and the bus driver watches over the bus. Passengers get on and off less frequently than on the train. While I don't feel comfortable sleeping unaccompanied on the train due to the potential of theft, this is less of a problem on coach buses. Generally, public transportation is extensive and convenient in Italy, particularly if traveling from one large city to another. Cities have well-developed urban bus lines, and major metropolitan areas may have metros and trams as well. In southern Italy, you will find that public transportation is less developed. Across the country, small towns and villages can be less accessible by train. If you have plans to travel extensively off the beaten path or in the southern half of the country, it can be helpful to have a car. Hiring a private driver is another approach if you're not sold on the idea of renting a vehicle.

Trains

It's the summer after my first year of college, and I'm backpacking in Europe with my brother. We decided to put our Eurorail passes to use and take a side trip from Rome to visit our relatives in L'Aquila. Located in relatively unspoiled Abruzzo, it is one of Italy's most beautiful and mountainous regions. I haven't seen them since I was twelve and am bursting with excitement. The train sets off with a few cars and passengers. After about an hour, it stops, and we need to exit and board a connecting train, *la coincidenza*. Switching trains is common when traveling to smaller cities. The train we board is comprised of only one carriage. The lights flicker every few minutes as we thunder through a series of seemingly endless tunnels. By the time we reach our destination, only one other passenger is left on board, a rail-thin man who looks to be in his nineties. Impeccably dressed in a suit and necktie, he reads the newspaper. My uncles Sesto, Salvatore, Olindo, and cousin Giannino are waiting for us at the train station with ear-to-ear grins. Giannino remarks that we will be famous as the first people since the Second World War who took the train from Rome to L'Aquila. He tells us that no one makes this trip by train anymore. It takes a circuitous route, twice as long as the bus, and its clamoring leaves your ears ringing.

Traveling by train is very popular with Italians and visitors to Italy. The lines connecting major cities, especially in northern and central Italy, are fast and efficient. Tickets can be purchased online, with your mobile phone, at a kiosk, or in person at the train station window. You can book a ticket on TrenItalia's official website (www.trenitalia.com) and find helpful information there about making reservations. In addition, a private company called Italotreno (www.italotreno.it/en) came onto the scene some years ago. From major airports like Milan's Malpensa or Rome's Fiumicino, they can be very convenient to get to the city center. However, visiting smaller cities, towns, and more remote destinations can be hit or miss.

HIGH SPEED OR FRECCE

Trains known as *frecce* (arrows), travel throughout Italy and can reach speeds of over 300 km (180 miles) per hour. They run straight into the heart of the most important cities, shortening travel times. Depending on the line, they may be called *Frecciarossa, Frecciargento,* or *Frecciabianca.* These are the nicest and most expensive categories of trains. Reservations are required before boarding, meaning your train ticket must be for a specific time and date.

INTERCITY

Intercity trains stop at around 200 large and medium-sized cities. They travel more slowly and stop frequently. They are excellent for reaching smaller towns. Or they can be a good option to save money when traveling to larger cities. Reservations are also required for intercity trains.

REGIONAL OR REGIONALE

Regionale trains transport passengers to larger and smaller cities and other locations that the *Frecce* and Intercity trains don't go to. They stay within the same region as opposed to getting from Rome to Napoli, for example. They might be busy in the mornings and around lunchtime on school days, as children often take the *Regionale* to get to school, and these trains are usually older and not as well-maintained. I've been on *Regionale* trains where the windows are bolted shut, and the air-conditioning didn't work, a bad combination in July. If you're traveling a long distance, stay away from the *Regionale,* unless you want a potentially uncomfortable adventure. At the same time, *Regionale* trains are convenient for getting to smaller towns cheaply. Though you are subjecting yourself to Italian roulette, picking a destination randomly and hopping off to explore can be interesting. When I was a student in Italy, one of my favorite things to do on a free weekend was make my way to the train station with an overnight bag, select a nearby town on the board, and see what happened. While reservations are not required for these regional trains, tickets must be validated before boarding.

VALIDATING TICKETS

For *Regionale* trains, as with municipal buses, and trams, tickets are not for any designated time. This is convenient because you can use your ticket when needed. But since it's open-ended, you must validate it before traveling. For trains, you'll notice little boxes with a space to insert your ticket near the train tracks. A few minutes before you board, slide either end of the ticket into the slot, and it should print the validation information. On buses and trams, you will also notice a box on board to validate tickets. As soon as you board, validate the ticket. If the machine is broken, tell an employee before they come to you to check the ticket. Otherwise, you may be subject to a fine.

STRIKES

Public transportation strikes are common. Usually, they will be announced in advance. Even during strikes, there are some guaranteed essential services. To find these, check the Italian Ministry of Transportation website on planned strikes. (scioperi.mit.gov.it/mit2/public/scioperi) If the train is on strike, improvise. Make an alternate plan or look at other options, like using the bus for intercity travel. This may even be more convenient. When I lived in Milan, I frequently opted for the bus over the train, which took me from northern Italy to the southern region of Abruzzo without having to make any connections as I would have with this train route.

PURCHASING TRAIN TICKETS

I generally use Trenitalia's official app, which I find useful when taking one of the high speed *frecce*. Since these trains require reservations, you will want to do this a least a few days in advance. If you go out further than a few months, the window to purchase may not be open yet. If you prefer to have a physical ticket, they can be bought in train stations at the ticket window or at automatic ticket machines. Purchasing your ticket at a self-service kiosk will be quicker unless you have a specific question to address at the counter. The queue at the counter can be extremely long during busy times.

The advantage of getting a physical regional ticket is that it can be purchased without a fixed date and time printed. You can buy a few in advance and take whichever train arrives first. However, if there is no set date and time indicated on it, you must validate your ticket. *Regionale* tickets can usually be purchased at the train station's *bar* especially if it is a small, regional location, some *tabaccherie* (shop that sells tobacco and many odds and ends) and *edicole* (newsstands). The smallest local train stations might not have an open ticket window. Another option is to use a travel agency, which are part of the landscape of most Italian towns. You'll pay a small fee, but you can avoid the lines and can ask the clerk if you have questions about your travel arrangements.

THE RIGHT TRAIN STATION

Even smaller cities have multiple train stations. Make sure you review in advance and purchase an appropriate ticket that takes you to the central railway station or place you want to reach. If it's a smaller station, you might take a *freccia* train to reach the main station, then get off and board another train or take the metro or a taxi after you arrive. If you select Rome, you will see Roma Termini and Roma Tiburtina listed first, then a list of many other Rome stations that follow. Note that the high-speed trains only stop at the major stations.

BOARDING THE RIGHT TRAIN

It can be a mad dash to board when your train arrives at the *binario* (platform). Italian trains are often late, and the *binario* might switch at the last minute. It's helpful to understand a few words from the loudspeaker or ask an employee if in doubt. To double-check with an employee, you can point to the train and say, "*È questo il treno per Roma?*" Is this train going to Rome?

Reading Transportation Schedules

Reading the transportation schedules may be a challenge if you are not used to the 24-hour clock or military time. For those unfamiliar with this system, try putting your phone and electronic devices in this format several weeks before you leave for Italy. In my opinion, it's a better system, as you will never confuse 8:30 am with 8:30 pm on a schedule, as 8 pm would be 20:00. Once you get to 12 noon, the numbers don't reset to 1 pm. They keep going until twenty-four hours or the day is up. Everything restarts at midnight when it's 0:00. To convert this to the system that uses am and pm, subtract twelve hours once you reach 13:00. In this book, I refer to time in this way to help you get accustomed.

Train stations have large charts on the wall that list the routes. These are helpful as they allow you to see all the locations that trains travel to from that station. The final destination will be listed in bold print at the top. Below the main destination are additional places where the train stops along the way and when it is scheduled to arrive at these towns. The chart also lists the *binario* (platform) the train typically departs from. It may also show the word *circola* (operates) and list days of the week or a time of year, necessary information when you're trip planning. Many stations also have an electronic version of this chart in a prominent location. It's essential to keep your ears tuned as occasionally there will be an announcement that the train is leaving from a different platform or is arriving *in ritardo* (late). This is an excellent reason to know Italian numbers and basic travel vocabulary.

Various types of transportation schedules have another enigma. You'll notice that some bus or ferry schedules (*battello, nave, traghetto, aliscafo* in Italian depending on the speed of the boat) include the words *feriali, festivo,* or *scolastico. Feriali* are working days, which are all days of the year except Sundays. Monday-Saturday are *feriale* days. However, *feriali* can become *festivi* if a holiday falls on one of those days. *Festivo, which* sounds like the word *festa,* is a public holiday or feast day. Italy considers all Sundays, feast days, and government holidays, to be *festivi.* In the supplemental materials, I've included a list of the major Italian holidays. *Scolastico* denotes when schools are in session. While Italian schools are in session on Saturdays, they would not be in August, for example. If you're confused, you are not alone. I've even had native Italians come up to me while waiting for a bus to ask for help deciphering the system. If a bus stops, even if it's not yours, it never hurts to ask the driver. I usually double-check upon boarding and ask whether the bus stops at the location I'm trying to reach. This tactic has saved me from ending up in the wrong place more than a few times.

Taxis

Generally, in Italy you can't hail a taxi, which are white in color and have a Taxi sign on top of the vehicle. You must call to reserve one or go to a taxi stand. You will not be expected to tip a taxi driver, but it's common to round up to the next euro. It's a good idea to take note of the taxi number and understand base rates for trips, such as the fare to and from the airport (for example, tourists have been charged €200—several times the flat rate in Rome). Taxis are also required to use their meters. You can verify this upfront with the driver and let them know you will need a receipt. I've also heard of instances where individuals have handed €50 to a driver and the driver told them they only gave them €20. To be on the safe side, pay attention during the transaction and review the money with them as you hand it over.

While Uber can be rare, an app called FREE NOW is a licensed ride-hailing app, owned by BMW Group and Daimler AG. It is in the English language and calls a local taxi, but you may not be able to pay with a credit card. In rural areas, these services are limited, so plan on organizing a ride.

Local Bus, Tram, and Metro

Local bus systems are generally well-developed throughout Italy, although schedules can be infrequent and out of the way in smaller towns. Many cities have trams, or street cars, and subway systems, known as the metro. Expect to buy the ticket before you board. These can be purchased at a *tabaccheria* (see Chapter VIII, Shopping) and some bars offer this service. Many news and magazine stands sell local bus and metro tickets. Don't forget to validate your ticket in a little box on the bus as soon as you board. Note that tickets have an expiration time of 60-90 minutes once validated.

Taking a local bus can be an inexpensive, adventurous way to see a village or smaller neighborhood away from the bustle of a larger metropolitan area. Having an exit plan and knowing which bus you'll take back is recommended. It's always a little gamble, but it will immerse you with the locals and take you to less-traveled destinations. While many areas outside of cities are safe, it's a good idea to travel as a pair and research. Particularly if you are exploring the neighborhoods outside of a larger city, you don't want to end up in an undesirable part of town.

Private Vehicles

Sometimes, it can be nearly impossible to get to a remote destination without a car. I've stayed in beautiful, out of the way places, then bounced around to multiple villages in a day, thanks to a car rental. Or when transiting from one major city to another, it can be an adventure to stop at little towns along the way. While it may be liberating, there are some key points to know. You may end up with a manual (stick shift) transmission or pay more for an automatic. If you're a driving abroad novice, central hill towns, the precipices of the Amalfi Coast, and the peaks of the Dolomites are not the places to learn. When driving into towns and cities, the roads can be exceptionally congested and have rules limiting traffic in certain places. You will notice signs indicating ZTL or Zona Traffico Limitato (Limited Traffic Zones), where only residents or authorized vehicles can enter. These zones can be monitored by cameras and you may not even know you violated a ZTL or received a speeding ticket, for that matter, until months later when the rental company charges your credit card. In general terms, I'd equate Italian driving to espresso drinking and queuing in line: it can be very fast and chaotic, with sometimes impatient drivers who have no qualms about tailgating you. Another issue you may encounter is limited parking in cities.

When you pick up your car, getting it from and returning it to an airport is a simple option, but you'll want to make sure you book well in advance, especially during the peak season. Italy's toll highway, called the *autostrada*, is a network of approximately 3,000 km (1,800 miles). Its official website (www.autostrade.it) allows you to check tolls, which can be pricey. Travel from Rome to Milan will cost more than €40 and the cost of fuel is nearly twice that of US prices. If you do travel the highways, I suggest you try eating at an Autogrill, where you'll find affordable high-quality espresso, panini, salads, treats, and often in a regional food shop with local specialties as well as a clean bathroom. The US State Department recommends that American tourists intending to drive in Italy obtain an International Driving Permit (IDP), which you can get through the American Automobile Association (AAA). It the case of US licensed drivers, it may be unlikely that you will be required to present it when renting a car, but it may come in handy if you get into an accident or have a legal encounter.

The Vespa has been featured in films such as the 1950s film *Roman Holiday*, where Audrey Hepburn tools around Rome on the classic moped. More recently, the animated film *Luca* chronicles the tale of two best friends, who also happen to be sea monsters, on their journey to win enough money to buy a Vespa. For long-term visitors, a scooter can be very convenient for short trips around town which is why they are ubiquitous. You can rent one for the day or longer periods of time. They can be fun for sightseeing in cities or on country roads, but it's not a form of transportation that should be used for long distances. They don't exceed 45 km/h (less than 30 mph) and they definitely cannot travel on major highways.

VIII

Shopping

*Italian style is a natural attitude. It is about a life of good
taste. It doesn't have to be expensive. Simple but with good
taste. Luxury is possible to buy. Good taste is not.*
—DIEGO DELLA VALLE

Italy is known for its specialty shopping, which can be quite personal. As Beppe Severgnini put it, in his book *La Bella Figura, A Field Guide to the Italian Mind*, "Fashion thinks it is sensuous, but other kinds of shopping in Italy is even more so. People want to look inside a table lamp, touch a suitcase, listen to an explanation, sniff a carpet, or sneak an olive and talk about the flavor." In this chapter, I'll describe some of the main categories of shops you'll encounter for items from clothing to artisan goods, medicines, fancy soaps, and just about everything in-between, along with the cultural protocols you can expect. Before delving into the content, I'll point out that shopping in Italy really comes in two different varieties. The first, I would call window shopping. In this circumstance, people wander the streets as they enjoy browsing clothes, bags, home goods, or other objects on display in the *vetrina* (shop window). Usually, signs listing the prices can be seen from the street. From that information, Italians enter a boutique relatively confident they will purchase an item. This is because the window displays are designed to provide a nearly perfect sense of what's inside and the price points. But what if there isn't a price listed on the items in the window of a boutique, you may ask. This usually means it's a very upscale shop. If you have to ask how much it costs, you probably don't have any business going into the store. The second type of shopping in Italy is what we would call the *entrata libera/ingresso libero* or free entrance. This doesn't mean you must pay to enter shops that don't display it. Instead, this phrase signals that you are encouraged to come inside just to browse. Casual looking is more common in tourist shops and large department stores like UPIM (Unico Prezzo Italiano Milano), or chains such as Flying Tiger Copenhagen, which sells toys, accessories, and gifts.

I Negozi (The Shops)

By and large, expectations once you enter a *negozio* are quite similar. So rather than go into a tedious explanation of each type of shop you might encounter, I will highlight a few and discuss broad-based cultural norms. With the occasional exception of some chains, large stores, and perhaps shopping centers found outside the city center, when you enter small and medium-sized shops, the assistant or clerk will almost immediately greet you with *buongiorno* or *buonasera*, depending on the time of day. Or *ciao* may be used among younger individuals. Follow their lead and return the same greeting. After that, they'll ask you if they can help you. If you're undecided, you can use this phrase to ask if you can browse, "*Posso dare un'occhiata?*" (Can I have a look around?) The shop assistant will usually say something like "*Certo*" (Of course, go right ahead) and indicate that you can let them know when you're ready for help. So, you have a look around, and let's say you see an item you'd like to examine further. Before you go over and pick it up, get their attention and ask "*Posso?*" (Can I?) If the assistant isn't looking in your direction, you can say, "*Scusi*" (Pardon me). Either they will say something like *certo*, or they will come over and help you with it. Tourists aren't always very good with these rules so you will often see "do not touch" signs or in Italian, *non toccare*.

One of the aspects I love about the service in Italy is that the shopkeepers are incredibly knowledgeable, and you can expect outstanding service. They have an intimate sense of what's in their shop. With clothing, for example, they seem to have a magical ability to glance at you, and almost immediately discern the size that will flatter your features. Perhaps because of this, it is a faux pas and considered rude to start handling the items. This is especially true in smaller boutiques, where clients don't enter to browse. In this setting, the shopkeeper might even follow around an undecided customer, saying *"Ah bellissimi"* (Really beautiful) or *"Questo colore è proprio bello"* (This color is stunning). In the case of shoes, you should rely on the shop assistant to retrieve the appropriate size and never try on shoes without help. Also, trying on shoes just for fun isn't a good idea. If you know you won't buy them, don't try them on. Note that small souvenir shops that sell kitschy items are usually a little less particular than more expensive shops. And if they are used to many tourists, you might even be ignored.

You can almost always pay with cash or a credit card. However, certain types, like American Express and Discover Card, are not widely accepted. While engaging in a bit of haggling at outdoor markets is acceptable, attempting this in a shop is poor etiquette. The best you could do is say, *"Se prendo più di uno si può fare lo sconto?"* (If I buy a few would you be willing to give me a discount?) However, they may do this automatically if you're pleasant and courteous and try to use some Italian or initiate a friendly conversation with them. I've had this happen a few times in the shop. The price might be €25, and the shopkeeper says, *"Facciamo €20"* (Let's do €20). Other times you might find that they will offer you a discount for a cash price. It can be challenging to return purchases to shops in Italy. This can be particularly awkward at small boutiques, whereas it should be easier with the receipt at large department stores. If you have saved the receipt, you might be able to exchange your stuff, but only within a limited period (one or two weeks, usually). I encourage you to take the Italian approach: when you buy something, be sure it's what you want, and don't look back. Another aspect to pay attention to is your own appearance. When entering a shop, you should dress for the occasion. If you go into a shop looking sloppy, wearing a pair of sweatpants or old sneakers, there will be much less of a level of trust. You might be followed around by the shopkeeper, appearing concerned as if you'll steal or break something.

Italy is a country of artisans who take enormous pride in what they produce. When visiting an artisan's shop, be careful what you say about the items. Often the craftsman is also the shopkeeper, or a friend or family member is, so it's better to be kind in your comments about items. Along with the idea of artisans is that Italians tend to value quality and may purchase fewer but higher quality possessions for their wardrobes and homes. They recognize known brands and show them off, so you will pay a premium for them, or anything made in Italy. When you see a nice jacket or something that appears to be a steal, it's highly possible it's not made in Italy. When it is, this aspect is usually prominently displayed on the item. So, if you don't see it, presume it's made somewhere else. Scarves and neckties can make good gifts if you want made-in-Italy products. They're light, beautiful, high quality, often made with Italian silk, and don't take up a lot of space in bags.

Even purchasing something from a *profumeria* (shop with soaps and perfumes), can be an adventure in cultural engagement. Like shopping at a boutique, you'll be greeted and asked if you need assistance as soon as you go through the door. Unless it's a luxury shop, it's okay to grab the item you want and take it right up to the counter to pay. You can ask the clerk for help if you're looking for something specific. While goods like soaps and toothpaste can be bought in the supermarket, I prefer to support the smaller shops in town. When I'm staying in the city center, with many shops, I see this as an opportunity to interact with someone new, maybe strike up a conversation about our lives and learn about different products as well.

Many different types of *negozi* were covered in the food section of this book. But with the approaches outlined, you should be able to adapt to just about any situation. When in doubt, a basic formula to remember is to greet the shop assistant, explain what you need or why you've entered (browsing is a valid reason), and say goodbye when you leave. *Grazie* is always acceptable when parting, *Buongiorno* and *Buonasera* also work depending on the time of day.

Edicola

Known as a newsstand in English, the *edicola* has been an integral part of the Italian landscape for decades. Despite diminishing numbers in recent years, thousands still exist across the country, with the majority located in northern and central Italy. There are about just as many *edicole* in Italy as there are McDonald's restaurants in the US, for comparison. You can find newspapers, periodicals, and books at these stands, which may also have local transportation tickets, maps, souvenirs, cards, DVDs, toys, and even perfumes.

Tabaccheria

Not just for smokers, a *tabaccheria* is a tobacco store and much more. A large T sign outside identifies these stores. Sometimes a (coffee) bar also doubles as a *tabaccheria*. Besides tobacco products, you can purchase tickets for local buses and trains, some stationary items, matches and lighters (perhaps needed if you have an older gas stove), and add credit to a cell phone. These might be international calling cards or simply a *Ricaricard*. A *Ricaricard* allows you to add credit to an Italian phone. Postage stamps (*francobolli*) are also available at the *tabaccheria*. The Italian post office can epitomize Italian bureaucracy, so for these products I suggest you use the *tabaccheria* when possible, to avoid it. Beyond that, you can pay utility bills at this shop.

Pharmacies and Medicine

Pharmacies, or *farmacie*, are marked with a universal green cross, often lit up when open. Operating hours are generally Monday-Saturday between 8:00 am and 20:00 (or 8 pm in the evening), and it may close during lunch, between 13:00 and 16:00. Pharmacies are closed on national holidays and Sundays, but if you need medicine, don't worry. There is usually a *farmacia di turno* (pharmacy on duty), meaning that by law, pharmacies in the area take turns to ensure one is available at night and during holidays in the event of emergencies. In larger metros, it should be reasonably easy to find one, but this can be more difficult in a smaller community, where the area might comprise other regional districts. You can look them up online in the *Pagine Gialle* (Yellow Pages). Generally, the doors will be locked, and you may have to knock or call the number provided.

Pharmacies carry health and beauty products and some nutritious foods. Most of the medicine or products carried are behind the counter and customers queue for their opportunity to speak with the pharmacist. Rather than an inconvenience, this is an added level of service. Most pharmacists will speak some English, but using a translation app and bringing a dictionary or an Italian speaker is a good idea.

If you know what you need, great, but understand that your favorite product, brand, or medicine likely won't be there. Don't worry, and let the pharmacist know the issue you need help with. The pharmacist will provide a few options for different products or medicines. They seem to have access to various over-the-counter medicines and additional categories of effective pharmaceuticals that can be distributed without a physician's prescription. In my opinion, the quality of items can be very high. When you feel ill, relying on a pharmacist first can reduce the need for a doctor. However, while knowledgeable about medicines, they did not attend medical school, cannot write prescriptions, and are not substitutes when a consultation with a physician is necessary. Additionally, they will only recognize drug scripts provided by an Italian doctor. So, when bringing prescribed medicine from home, it can be helpful to have extra, otherwise, you may need to spend time and money to visit an Italian doctor to purchase your meds in Italy.

Aside from the stores already mentioned, here is a brief list of a few other shops and businesses you may frequently encounter:

Parrucchieria, a hair salon that serves women and sometimes men

Barbiere, a barber shop

Cartoleria, a stationery store that could also sell books, gifts, etc.

Libreria, a bookstore

Lavanderia, laundromat

Abbigliamento, a general term for clothing shop

Un Negozio di Biancheria, a store that specializes in undergarments and linens

Elettrodomestici, an electronics store

Ferramenta, a hardware store

Mesticheria, a store that sells items for the home and some hardware

Cash or Credit Card

Before the mass digitalization accelerated by the Covid-19 pandemic, some Italians might be reluctant or denied using a credit card to pay for a low-cost item, like a coffee. Post-pandemic, cards are much more accepted, particularly in cities. On my latest trip, I loaded my credit cards onto Apple Pay, which worked beautifully. Before the pandemic, this would have been inconceivable. I love paying this way because my phone is easily accessible, and there's no need to fumble with a wallet and cards. The Italian government has encouraged Italians in this way by adopting a lottery for merchants and customers who use cashless payment and reducing taxes for credit card purchases. Even so, I always advise carrying cash, especially in smaller towns, rural areas, and less economically developed regions. There are also still some stores that won't accept credit cards for purchases below €10, and if you try to buy a coffee with a large banknote, you may be asked if you have anything smaller. In the past, change was sometimes treated like a prize possession. It's still not entirely unusual for a cashier to ask, *"Hai moneta/spiccioli?"* (Do you have change?) I've watched clerks look wide-eyed upon me displaying a palm filled with pocket change. Then, they'd say, *"Ah, venti centesimi, perfetto!"* (Oh, twenty cents, perfect!). If you do need cash, cities and towns will have multiple ATMs, usually attached to a bank, and they offer the best exchange rates. However, they can be hard to locate in rural locations. As a sidenote, major airports in Italy are a convenient location to withdraw money. If I don't have any euros from a previous trip, I make sure to get some from an airport's ATM (*bancomat*) before leaving it. Anything other than an ATM (currency exchange counters, etc.) will typically give you a poor rate.

I suggest bringing two credit cards with you and at least one bank card that allows you to withdraw cash. Do research, as certain cards charge fees on international conversions. There are credit card companies, such as Capital One in the US, that claim to be fee-free. When traveling abroad, keep one card on you, leave one in a secure location, and try incorporating Apple Pay. In the event your card is stolen, you'll have an alternative. Regarding credit card transactions, Europeans would find it unacceptable for a server to take your credit card to run the transaction out of sight. In Italy, a waitperson or merchant should always bring a portable machine and conduct the transaction right in front of you. I appreciate this as it helps protect your information from being compromised. When using a credit or debit card, you may be asked, *"Bancomat?* (Is this a debit card? Note, this is the same word for ATM). You can either reply, *"Sì"* or *"No, carta di credito"* (Yes or No, credit card).

IX

Business in Italy

A well-maintained physique is a great business card. Ideas and intelligence are what matters, but if you have a well-maintained physique, it's better.
—Giorgio Armani

This section, primarily for business travelers and those who plan to be in Italy longer term, is intended to give you a brief overview of fundamental cultural differences in Italian business, as well as tips on how to operate in the context. Some of the content is based off an interview with Daniel Chiaravalli, who earned an MBA at Milan's SDA Bocconi University in the same class as me. It intentionally does not cover the structure of the Italian economy or nuances. The US Department of Commerce's Italy Country Commercial Guide provides an excellent summary of those topics. (www.trade.gov/italy-country-commercial-guide)

Daniel has Italian origins and part of his plan was to stay a few years to reclaim Italian citizenship. During the process, he was entrenched in Italian bureaucracy, which Daniel said, "can be a total nightmare." The process took nearly five years longer than anticipated. Still, it is not entirely surprising and is an excellent initial lesson to frame a discussion on doing business in Italy. Post-MBA, Daniel remained in Italy in a marketing role for the pharmaceutical industry, but two years later had no choice but to enroll in a second master's program to be legally permitted to work in the country. After that, he spent four years working for a large multinational pharmaceutical company in business development and key account management. It can be hard to make deep relationships, even for fluent Italian speakers with connections to the heritage. Italians will view you as an outsider and, unless you grew up together, you'll never penetrate their inner circles. Even among Italians, there is loyalty to their regional identities. Working with a local agent or translator who can make an introduction may help establish trust.

Regarding business presentations, they are not necessarily made in front of a group or seen as a public display where eye contact and embodying the persona of an engaging speaker matters. This would be seen in Italy as *americanata*, a pejorative meaning "excessively American in style." In Italian presentations, everyone sits down, and the presenter's seat is where they can most easily connect their computer to the projector. Presentations are much more standardized and formal, with basic facts about the company, its qualifications, and the value proposition. Meetings are often merely formalities; the decision to go forward is not made during presentations. These types of decisions happen during a coffee outside the meeting or a phone call between two executives. Since Italy is a hierarchical culture, having a senior executive at a meeting may go a long way in getting buy-in on a course of action.

An Italian CEO who came to speak to my MBA program mentioned the "three Cs" required to be successful in Italian business: *competenze, conoscenze, culo* (vulgar). This translates to *what you know, who you know, and luck.* This is an interesting segue into a discussion about the difference between Italian and English language proverbs and the climate. Even in professional settings, certain practices may appear to be offensive to a non-Italian, and in particular women. As a case in point, in Italian there is a saying, *"Non si può avere la botte piena e la moglie ubriaca,"* which means you can't have a full barrel and a drunk wife. In English, we might say, "You can't have your cake and eat it too." During a factory tour near Bergamo with some of my college students, they were shocked to see posters of pin-up girls hanging in workspaces. Italy is still, in some respects, a masculine work culture and it may not be unheard of to hear women objectified. However, this is not across the board, and work cultures vary greatly. As with anything, it's best not to make assumptions and be careful about crossing any lines yourself.

Meetings generally don't occur before 11 am, and colleagues don't get hung up on meeting times. For example, you might say, *"Ci vediamo verso le undici."* This means "See you around 11 am," a distinct difference in saying "at 11 am." Employees could arrive late and offer an excuse. Traffic is a common scapegoat, and this attitude may not be looked down upon. However, as a visitor, you should always be punctual. Also note that in northern Italy, meetings may be expected to start timelier than in the south. It is not advisable to propose a meeting at 8 am or 9 am as this is a social time for Italians. However, because lunch is usually at 1 pm, scheduling a meeting between 11 am to 1 pm makes sense, with participants often heading to lunch after. You may notice that people frequently interrupt each other in meetings and discussions. And you may need to insert yourself to convey your ideas.

Naturally, there is an important element of *la bella figura* in business, which I'll highlight here. However, you should refer to Chapter III, La Bella Figura, for more general information on this practice. Dressing well is essential, especially in Italy's fashion capital, Milan. While an Italian is shaking your hands, most likely they will take notice of your shoes, which should be polished. Not just the substance but the form is paramount. When pressed about how he defined well-dressed, Daniel said he wore a suit and necktie daily and that the traditional business suit is blue. Gray is also acceptable, while a black suit is reserved for lawyers. When in doubt, it's better to dress more conservatively. Even in summer months in the oppressive heat of Rome, you'll observe businesspeople in long-sleeved button-down shirts and suits. Formal American corporate dress is appropriate for women, erring on the conservative side and in muted colors. High-quality items are noticed and taken to indicate your status and show respect for the encounter. An important meeting is the time to display a nice watch or jewelry. Suits, shirts, jackets, pants, and dresses should be well-fitting, unwrinkled, and in a nice material. For example, cheap, fake leather shoes, belts, or poor-quality neckties may give the wrong impression. I travel with a bottle of wrinkle releaser and tend to steam my clothes in the shower before an important meeting. Even in less formal situations, I always travel with a sports coat in Italy. And your behavior should match the formality, using titles instead of first names.

Paolo, an Italian expat who I got to know while he was pursuing a master's degree at Penn State a decade ago, has had a successful career working at major players in consulting and the tech industry. He lives on the west coast of the United States and had some advice for doing business with Italians. Having been on the receiving end of stereotypes, he cautions against bringing them into your professional relationships. It can be highly offensive to imply that Italians are lazy or that business lunches are always hours long. In addition, offhand comments that denigrate Italians into a caricature could be highly offensive. To avoid a faux pas, avoid joking about Italians and don't state any generalizations about Italians. It may be offensive to conflate all Italians with those from different regions.

With holidays, be aware of the *"ponte,"* meaning bridge, in Italian. Midweek holidays often extend (or are bridged) through the weekend. During the week of August, known as Ferragosto, Italians take summer vacations, and it is best to avoid this period all together when conducting business. Latin expressions are fairly common in business and there is one that is applicable here, *"In medio stat virtus,"* meaning that virtue lies in the middle, or that we should practice moderation. This epitomizes the idea that Italians value their time off; they are conscious of not overworking and enjoying personal time. Rushing a project or proposal or being forceful about a timeline could be off-putting to an Italian colleague. Nudging or asking about their status is okay, but diplomacy is essential. Business is nuanced, and you must influence the right people rather than expecting an instant decision. If you use pressure tactics, you may get polite pushback. Even though you want to avoid being seen as rushing the process, responses to their inquiries should be prompt. When making an initial request, opening up with an email in Italian will likely lead to a quicker reply, which may even transition to communication in English.

Concerning meals, they have a critical social and business function. You're likely to notice a midmorning coffee break that may be a walk to a local bar or a gathering around the machine, depending on what's available. Business lunches begin around 1-2 pm, and around 3 pm, you may go out together for another coffee. These are all opportunities to leverage critical social time to construct relationships. When the workday ends around 5-6 pm, it's possible you may go for an *aperitivo*. Business dinners could begin at 8 pm or even as late as 10 pm in the south. If you are invited to a meal, it's customary for your host to pay. Still, it is good etiquette for you to offer to pay, but don't insist. You should, however, take care of the bill when you invite a counterpart out for a meal. If you are invited to someone's home, a quality wine or dessert can be an appropriate gift. You may ask if they will have seafood or meat, as the former would require white wine, while red wine is consumed with meat. Gifts are not necessary for business. If you do bring gifts, something high quality and unique from your home country is a safe bet. (See Chapter III, La Bella Figura, for more on gift giving.)

When unsure how to approach a business situation, it's best to follow the lead of your counterpart abroad rather than launch into a discussion about your objectives. Social but professional conversations typically precede a meeting. Understand some aspects of Italian culture or the region where you are visiting. These topics would be fitting to bring up as you get to know each other. I'd advise that you are complimentary about Italy, stay away from politics, and avoid mentioning any poor impressions of Italy or negative experiences you had during your stay.

X

Practical Matters

Tra il dire e il fare c'è di mezzo il mare.
(An ocean lies between what is said and what is done.)
—ITALIAN PROVERB

Communication While Home and Abroad

When traveling to Italy, it makes sense to bring a smartphone with you as it will work as a Wi-Fi device for no fee. Check with your carrier ahead of your travels, as many offer affordable data plans or day passes for a fee. Suppose you're in Italy for a more extended period. You might purchase an Italian phone or SIM card, presuming your phone is unlocked and accepts one. Then, you can buy credit or a phone plan. Another option is purchasing a basic phone in Italy, which might be worth considering if you make many voice calls. The store clerk will register your information if you're buying a phone number, which requires your passport.

Most phones will automatically work abroad, so if you do not enable a phone plan and fail to turn off your data, you will be charged at the provider's rates, which could be multiples of what you typically pay. This is true for calls and data usage. You could be charged even if you do not answer, but your voicemail does. If data is a must, consider a portable hotspot like Skyroam. Voice calls can be made with data through Skype, WhatsApp, and many others. Skype can be used to call a landline, although you will have to purchase credit, which comes at a low cost. When communicating within Italy, you may use WhatsApp to make reservations or even communicate via Instagram messaging.

Here is what I'd suggest concerning phone service:

Check with your carrier to determine how to adjust your phone plan for Italy or Europe.

Turn off data and roaming when you're not using it.

Use the Wi-Fi capabilities of your phone when a network is available.

Making and Receiving Calls

Calling from Italy to Another Country

United States/Canada: Dial: 00 + 1 + (area code) + (7-digit phone number).

Note that 00 is the prefix to make a call from Italy to another country, and 1 is the country code to call the US and Canada.

Australia: Dial 00 + 61+ (area code) + phone number

United Kingdom: Dial 00 + 44 + (area code) + phone number

Ireland: Dial 00 + 353 + (area code) + number

To call anywhere else from Italy, you dial 00 + (international country code) + (area code) + (phone number).

Calling Italy from Another Country

United States/Canada: 011 + 39 + the local number

Australia: 0011 011 + 39 + the local number

United Kingdom: 00 +39 + the local number

Ireland: 00 +39 + the local number

Note that 39 is the code to call Italy from another country.

Making a Call within Italy

Dial the local number. No code is necessary.

Landline numbers start with 0, and cell phones start with 3.

Emergency Numbers in Italy

Dial the following numbers with no codes:

112: If there is an emergency and you are unsure who to call. This single emergency number should have an English-language answering service. It routes to the Carabinieri, Italy's national police, although directly reaching a local number may result in receiving help more promptly.

113: Will connect you to the Polizia di Stato, or State police, which can also be used for general emergencies.

115: This will connect you to the fire department for a fire or suspected gas leak.

118: If there is a medical emergency, this will connect you with an ambulance service.

Electricity and Plugs

Italian plug sockets will be different than what you have at home. They accept two or three round prongs, rather than the two flat rectangular prongs used in the US. You can pick up an adapter that allows your appliance to fit into the wall socket but beware that electricity in Europe is 220-240 volts (in the US it's 110 volts). If you plug a 110-volt hair dryer into an Italian plug, it will burn up. This could potentially blow out power in your apartment or hotel. Suppose you require a particular electronic device like hair dryers, straighteners, curling irons, etc. In that case, there are some options: leave it at home, purchase one in Italy, or buy a voltage converter. It converts the electricity flowing into the device into the proper voltage. Also, check whether your device can accommodate European voltage (check the electrical specifications on your appliance). Computers and phone chargers are typically equipped to convert the voltage. You will likely only need an adapter to convert your plug into the round prongs.

Legal Differences

While, thankfully, most tourists do not end up in the Italian criminal justice system, I still think it's essential to know some basic information. As Benjamin Franklin said, "An ounce of prevention is worth a pound of cure." I am not a lawyer, and this is not legal advice, but it is intended to provide you with some basic guidelines on potential legal issues and differences you may encounter in Italy. You should review the US Department of State webpage on Italy (travel.state.gov) for updated information before traveling. Consult an international lawyer for counsel if you have specific legal questions. The bottom line is that you do not want to get into legal trouble abroad, but if you are arrested, ask the authorities to contact your local Consulate or Embassy immediately.

The foundational concept to remember when traveling to another country is not to assume that laws are the same as they are at home. If you understand US law, you likely have heard about the right to life, liberty, the pursuit of happiness, freedom of speech, and freedom of expression. These principles are also present in the Italian system, which is guided by a constitution. I interviewed Italian Attorney Federico Antich, who practices law in Florence and specializes in international law. He pointed out some legal and cultural concepts in Italian law that may be familiar and foreign to visitors. While in the US, there is a presumption of innocence until proven guilty, Article 27 of the Italian Constitution provides that "the defendant is not considered guilty until finally convicted." This is significant because it was designed for preemptive detention, meaning that law enforcement can hold you for forty-eight hours before your circumstances are reviewed by a judicial authority.

Additionally, the prosecutor can use the time you are being preliminarily held to gather evidence to decide whether to bring you to court. If you get into legal trouble, there is no option to pay bail to be released from prison or detained until the trial. In some cases, defendants could be held for long periods, even years. In addition, should you be put on trial, the outcome is not determined by a jury of your peers. Defendants are found guilty or innocent by a judge.

Another difference is that the right to bear arms does not exist in Italy, and even carrying a knife for self-defense can be problematic. Regarding driving while intoxicated, in recent years Italy has had instances of vehicular deaths caused by foreigners, in some cases without licenses. In response, penalties for vehicular homicide and operating a vehicle under the influence are severe. Of course, visitors are much more likely to end up with minor traffic violations, such as tickets for driving into a historic center or speeding.

Italian law requires that you carry identification. If you are a non-EU Citizen, the only valid identification will be your passport. A photocopy may be helpful with merchants or others. But, with authorities, it is not an acceptable form of identification and has no legal value. If you are stopped by police, you will be expected to show them your official identification upon request. Federico indicated that if you can't provide this valid identification to the police officer, they could legally argue that you are trying to hide your identity, in which case you might be held at a police station until the situation is sorted out. In a worst-case scenario, you could be held for a few hours or even overnight in jail while your identity is determined. If you are stopped, it's expected that you will tell the officer why you are in Italy and where you are staying. This information lets them know that you are legally in the country and have plans to return to your home country. It never hurts to have a copy of your return ticket itinerary ready, whether this is in a digital or printed format. From my own experience, I've been asked this, especially when entering the country. If you overstay your visa, you will be considered an illegal immigrant, subject to immediate deportation. You could also be subject to a €5,000-10,000 fine and may have issues returning to Italy.

Should you be stopped by police, remain calm and be polite. The officer's ability to communicate well in English may be an issue, and it is not unheard of for tourists to be accompanied to the police station by an Italian-speaking friend or local contact who then translates for the authorities.

Regarding those with dual citizenship, how you enter the country makes a difference. If you enter Italy with an Italian passport, legally you will be looked at as Italian. This may have implications should you need the US government for support while abroad. But if you enter with a US passport, for example, you will be viewed as an American citizen. Federico said that shuffling passports can be tricky and may raise red flags with authorities if they detect something inconsistent. If you are the holder of an additional passport, carefully research the implications of entering and exiting with these documents. Consult an attorney for legal advice.

Note that Italian law requires that hotels, lodging structures, apartments, and even campsites provide public authorities with information on guests daily. Otherwise, the business is subject to fines or other sanctions. For a foreigner, you will be asked for your passport to record these details. While in the US, only the individual responsible for the room is typically required to present identification; in Italy, this extends to all guests. Furthermore, the rate changes if you add an additional person. Additionally, some cities require lodging structures to collect a daily tax that can range from €1-7, depending on the city and star rating of the accommodation, which is collected directly by the business.

On the Beach

Cassandra Santoro operates tours for hundreds of visitors a year on the Amalfi coast. She pointed out that Americans tend to bring chairs and umbrellas to the beach and may not be accustomed to renting them, which is customary in Italy. Additionally, even though beaches are public land in Italy, you can't always access them. Visitors do not claim a spot for free by simply sprawling out a towel in the sand. There are free beaches in Italy, but in many popular coastal areas the majority of the beaches are beach clubs (known as *stabilimenti, bagni,* or *lido*) that are managed by private companies who tightly pack the prime real estate with rows of colorful umbrellas and sunbeds. If you head to a beach that offers umbrellas and chairs for rent, you will be expected to pay a fee and will also have access to amenities such as a lock box, toilet, shower, and lifeguard in some cases. Some beach clubs have a restaurant or café that sells food and drinks to beachgoers. Italians may even rent a beach hut for as many as six people for the week or an entire season, which is an annual tradition for some families.

Depending on the upscale nature of the location and the time of year, it may cost anywhere between €25-100 a day to rent an umbrella and two beach chairs. The regions of Puglia and Sardinia by law guarantee a percentage of free beaches as well as spectacular settings. They may be good places to look if you are interested in saving money, but you will not have access to the services a club offers. As Italy has a warm Mediterranean climate, Italians are unlikely to go to the beach for swimming unless it is summer and hot. If you tolerate the cold, there's nothing wrong with splashing around in the ocean in April, although the locals might shake their heads a little.

Trash and Recycling

According to Cassandra Santoro, understanding the garbage is vital for people in apartments and B&Bs. She says, "If you do not understand how the garbage works, it sits there, and that's when (you start to get) bugs, and the city gets dirty." Italy has high standards for recycling and sustainability. Cassandra found that in her experience living on the Amalfi coast, its residents are proud of the sanitation. There is a system where they throw away different items, such as plastic, on Monday and separate all recyclables, even returning garbage if something is mixed in that shouldn't be. In my time in Italy, I observed this with the Airbnb host presenting me with a chart to explain the procedures. The issues with the trash are Airbnb's most significant problem on the Amalfi coast.

Italy is a small, concentrated country, and it can create major environmental issues when tourists don't adhere to local procedures. If necessary, take a few minutes to ask how to dispose of trash, be respectful, and help minimize pollution in Italy.

Toilets

A restroom break is not always straightforward in Italy. First, it can be a challenge to find a public restroom, although those located in tourist areas are often indicated by "WC," an abbreviation for the antiquated term water closet. Some public restrooms are free of charge and others require you to pay 50 cents or €1, so it can be handy to carry a few coins with you. Often the best strategy is to enter a coffee bar or café and make a small purchase, as you can't expect to use the facilities at an eatery unless you are a customer. Restrooms at restaurants, bars, and other establishments may not have separate rooms for men and women, meaning you will wait your turn. Sometimes there is a different restroom for each gender, but a shared sink area. Potential places where you might be able to access a restroom free of charge are fast food chains such as McDonald's and potentially train stations, but some will charge a fee. Trains are equipped with restrooms for passengers to use during travel. Museums, so long as you've paid to enter, will also typically have facilities available.

Hygienic standards for public toilets are extremely inconsistent and may be much lower than your expectations. It's common for the toilet bowl not to include a seat and for there to be no toilet tissue. Another oddity is occasionally a toilet is merely a ceramic hole in the ground, known as a squat toilet. When you go to wash your hands, you may find the faucet doesn't work and the paper towels and soap haven't been restocked. Because of this, many travelers bring a travel size package of tissues and hand sanitizer. Flushing mechanisms and how the sink works sometimes perplex visitors. If you don't see a faucet to turn on the water, look at the ground. There may be a sink pedal or what appears to be a ball of rubber protruding from the floor that you step on to operate the water. When flushing, there may be two different sized buttons on a toilet. The larger button releases more water if necessary. If you cannot locate a flushing mechanism on the toilet, there may be a pull chain or foot pedal.

Value Added Tax (IVA)

Note that prices in Italy include value-added tax (VAT) or Imposta sul Valore Aggiunto (IVA) in Italian, a consumption tax that businesses must collect on the government's behalf. It is already included in the price of goods and services. It will not be added to your credit card later, as all prices displayed include IVA. The standard IVA rate of tax in Italy is 22 percent, but there are lower rates for certain goods and services. For example, food, drinks, and agricultural products are assessed at 4 percent. Fortunately, visitors who reside outside can be refunded a portion of the tax included in the price if it exceeds €154.94 (VAT included) at the time of this writing. Some shops, particularly in heavy tourist areas, will advertise tax-free options, or you can ask. They will need to see a copy of your passport. It's essential to keep your receipts to document the purchase. There are also tax-free processors, such as Global Blue, that have booths in cities and in airports. Goods may need to be inspected and in new condition to qualify for the refund.

Visiting Museums and Cultural Sites

United Nations Educational, Scientific and Cultural Organization (UNESCO) World Heritage Sites are sites designated important to the world's cultural or natural heritage. Italy tops this list with more than 58 UNESCO sites, and reviewing these will give you a great insight into the country's cultural heritage. Many of these represent archaeological areas such as Pompei and Ercolano, or the Roman mosaics beautifully preserved at Villa Romana del Casale at Piazza Armerina, Sicily. Others are historic city centers or monuments.

There is also no shortage of museums to visit, and while many artistic masterpieces are consolidated in famous galleries, you'll also find breathtaking frescos in churches and palaces. While some are famous, like the Doge's Palace in Venice, the heritage is so incredibly rich, chances are there are many artistic treasures in even any small town you visit that are also worth exploring. If you're intent on visiting more popular museums, such as the Galleria dell'Accademia in Florence, which houses Michelangelo's sculpture of David, here are a few tips:

Review the schedule and make sure the museum is open the day you are planning to be in town.

Note that museums are often closed on Mondays and typically are open around 9 am-7 pm but may vary.

Many well-known museums require you to purchase tickets in advance, and times may sell out quickly during the peak season, so book early.

Be prepared to check your bag or backpack or leave it in your room as they can be prohibited.

Museums may have a dress code that requires you to have your shoulders and knees covered, which is especially true for churches or religious sites.

Before taking any photos make sure you check if it's permitted.

XI

Safety

*Safety is something that happens between your ears, not
something you hold in your hands.*
—JEFF COOPER

As I begin this section, I'll point out that Italy is a country where
violent crime is rare. Many visitors won't ever encounter problems.
The US State Department website (travel.state.gov), which I consider required reading before your travels, mentions that Italy experiences moderate economic crime and theft. While I think it's
always advisable to practice vigilance, circumstances vary greatly.
As you educate yourself and begin understanding potential problems, you'll understand when to relax or be more alert. This section
isn't to scare you but to help you develop some awareness, reduce
the likelihood that you will be a victim of petty thefts, and minimize the potential for more serious, although less likely, situations.

Sonny Smith of Sixsightco (sixsight.co) has a passion for personal safety and agreed to connect with me on this topic. A former
Royal Marine Commando and ex-member of the British Special
Forces, who now offers self-defense training and works as a body-
guard, including experience in Italy, he has an impressive resume.
Sonny suggested that travelers have some basic familiarity with
their environment before they even leave home. One approach is
to check out Google Earth and Google Street View, as well as go
on Instagram and type in the hashtag of a location. This can give
you confidence in navigating an unfamiliar city, which could be

quite useful upon arrival. It could also give you some insights into how locals dress, which may help you to avoid standing out. (See clothing in Chapter III, La Bella Figura.) A fun way to approach this is to pack light and fill in the gaps in your wardrobe with items purchased abroad. The main reason it's better not to stand out is to avoid attracting the attention of pickpockets, which are very common in tourist destinations.

Regarding displays of wealth, as a general guideline, you are better off not wearing expensive jewelry or displaying a designer bag. This varies by location to some extent and is particularly true in cities, transportation stations, and areas that have many tourists. When I went to Naples, I decided not to wear my watch when I heard that a thief had taken a Rolex right off a friend's wrist. Tourists are perceived as having money. Looking wealthier than others can make you a more attractive target. So, while Italians tend to be well dressed, they usually aren't overly fancy unless going out for a nice dinner or to a special event. My advice is to look well-put-together but conservative in your appearance.

Embassy and Consulate Information

Another smart move is to ensure you have the essential contact information for your home government. Keep the phone numbers and addresses of your embassy or consulate in an accessible location, in addition to entering them in your phone. While most travelers may not need them, it will complicate matters if you get into trouble and don't have it. US citizens should utilize the Smart Traveler Enrollment Program (STEP), signing up online through the US State Department website. This service allows US citizens and nationals who travel overseas to register their trip with the nearest US Embassy or Consulate. Once enrolled, you will receive updates on safety and threats, and the program is helpful for emergencies.

Nightlife and Alcohol Consumption

Alcohol can pose a significant safety risk, especially for younger travelers and those who have limited experience with it. As discussed previously, when intoxicated you become a softer target for crime, and your judgment can be impaired. There is also the possibility of being drugged through food or drink that you consume. While uncommon, according to the US State Department, this does occur. Do not take food or drinks from a stranger, especially when out at night and traveling alone. Keep an eye on your glass, being extra cautious at crowded nightclubs or bars. It's not recommended to go out and drink alone, as contacts have told me unsuspecting visitors have been targeted and ingested Rohypnol (or Roofies) with severe consequences. If you visit a nightclub, you'll probably notice that Italians can be very friendly and may want to get to know you. If you meet an Italian while you're out for the evening, especially when alcohol is involved, proceed with caution. Regarding safety, you are better off getting a phone number and meeting them the next day in a public place, for something innocuous such as for lunch or in the piazza for a walk during the daylight. Preferably, have some friends come along, and don't trust those you meet immediately.

Pickpocketing and Thefts

As mentioned, petty thefts and pickpocketing are common in Italy. Be aware of distractions. If someone spills something on you, tries to help you with your bags, wants you to sign a petition, strikes up an invasive conversation, bumps into you, invades your personal space, etc., you're better off assuming it's a tactic to divert your attention. Tourists should also be cautious when there are street performers as it may be a diversion, noting that often thieves work in teams and seize the opportunity to work through a crowd. These may include street gangs from Eastern Europe, easily distinguished by their dress and ethnicity, as well as others who blend in with the crowd. I had a run-in with them when I was a kid while walking with my grandfather in Rome. Several would-be thieves closed in on us and thrust horizontally held newspapers into our bodies. The goal was to distract us while concealing their hands as they would soon rifle through our pockets. Fortunately, we recognized this and chased them off, but others are not so lucky.

Aside from tourist areas, the highest risk is in transportation stations in large cities. According to the US Department of State, most train station thefts are reported at Rome's Termini, Milan's Centrale, Florence's Santa Maria Novella, and Naples's Centrale at Piazza Garibaldi. In these areas, thieves are likely watching you. Travelers should pay particular attention on city buses in Rome and the metro, the Circumvesuviana train (between Naples and Sorrento). If you take out your phone and put it back in your pocket, presume that someone has noticed. Absolutely do not keep valuables in external pockets, and don't give the pickpockets a head start by revealing the location of your valuables. Busy Italian train stations can be chaotic, dirty, and risky for your bags. As a side note, vagrants hang out around these stations, which are usually located in a seedy area of the city. If possible, I would avoid staying near the train station and travel with a companion when in these areas. Predators sometimes appear to be ordinary or even well-dressed individuals. In large and medium-sized cities, never turn your back on your bags. If you wear a backpack, be aware that a hand can quickly get inside and probe around without you knowing. Some thieves have even been known to use a razor to cut into bags, so those little locks won't help. Don't keep valuables in your pack unless they remain in your line of sight and are in a hard-to-reach internal compartment. A huge mistake is keeping a wallet or phone in your back pocket. The thieves are talented, so you probably won't know when or where you lost your personal items.

I meticulously pack my bags before going through any busy tourist area or train station. I keep essential items in an internal zipper pocket of my clothing, opting for a vest or jacket, depending on weather conditions. When going through crowds, keep your hands in your pocket on your wallet or over your purse (in front of you).

If you carry a purse or bag, hedge your bets, and don't put all your valuables in it. Keep a credit card and some cash on your person, in another bag, or hidden in your room. If you have a money belt or travel pouch, wear it (under your clothes) when in busy tourist areas and on crowded public transportation. You can keep your passport, credit cards, and perhaps even your phone inside the pouch. Even when securing my valuables, I still tend to keep some cash in a pocket and potentially one credit card. That way, when it's time to pay for a coffee or train ticket, I don't have to reveal the location of my valuables. It's not a good idea to expose and rummage through a travel pouch in public. Do not be buried in your phone or wear headphones in tourist areas, in and around transportation stations, and when taking public transportation in cities.

A countermeasure to thievery is utilizing walls, which has been part of my toolkit for years. It can help protect your possessions and yourself. You might be familiar with the military terminology "watch your six," with six referring to the face of a clock. It means to watch your back, as it's where you're vulnerable. When you stand with your back against the wall or in a corner, a thief cannot approach you from behind. You can scan what's in front of you and to your sides. You'll be a more challenging mark than the tourist who stops in the middle of a crowd to look at their phone. You can implement this technique when waiting for transportation and in all public areas.

Additionally, stand with your bag tightly between your legs while at the train, metro, or bus stop rather than have it sit to your side, or keep a firm hand on it. When you are disoriented, vulnerable, and appear like an unsavvy tourist is when you become a target. You will stand out less if you appear confident and avoid dressing flashy. The goal is not to try to be Jason Bourne or put on a theatrical display mimicking some exaggerated Italian caricature, it's simply to blend in and appear like a less attractive target compared to others around you. Lastly, as is smart policy anywhere you go, don't leave valuables unattended in a vehicle, and certainly, don't leave items in the line of sight. If you are parked in a rough area, near a train station, or in a city, a thief might notice something in the window and do a quick smash-and-grab. You can't predict who might target your vehicle, even in upscale areas.

Security in your Lodgings

If staying in an apartment, only let people in the building that you know. Get into the habit of locking your doors when you return home and don't leave windows open unless they have external bars. If you're in a hostel or location where the door is not secure, Sonny suggests you could consider getting a door wedge with an alarm. This device is transportable and can help prevent a door from being opened. When tripped, it sets off a loud audio alarm, which can buy you time, alert others, and scare off an intruder. This is likely overkill in most places in Italy, but it's an option if you are anxious. As a word of caution, be guarded of anyone who comes to your door. During one stay in Umbria, I recall two men appearing at my apartment. They announced they were from the gas company and needed to look around the flat I was renting. It didn't feel right, so I apologetically closed the door on them and immediately called the landlord. She said this was unexpected and I was right to refuse them entry. Thieves and scammers have been known to invent excuses to enter homes. When in doubt, verify with your rental agency or landlord before letting workers inside.

Situational Awareness

It's always a good idea to be aware of your surroundings. Be extra cautious at night, especially if you are a female traveler. When possible, travel in groups of two or three and avoid walking in poorly lit alleys and side streets. If you do end up in a situation where you feel uncomfortable, try to exude confidence and give off a menacing vibe. Channel your favorite action hero's tough guy face, walk with a purpose, keep your head up, and get to a secure area.

When in bigger cities, near transportation stations, or in a dicey neighborhood, it doesn't hurt to be cautious when someone takes an interest in you. Ask yourself if this person seems like they have a reason to be here and whether they're acting naturally? If they don't seem to have a reason to be in the area and their behavior seems odd, you should be on alert. Trust your gut, and don't worry about ignoring people or seeming rude if you feel uncomfortable.

As a safety net in uncomfortable scenarios, you can use WhatsApp to alert others. Open a message to a selected contact and share your location. (It would be best if you worked out in advance that you will only do this to alert them of an emergency.) This allows you to notify someone who can help while communicating your whereabouts. Just make sure you don't linger on your phone and be mindful to remain mentally present. You can utilize your phone's built-in SOS feature in a genuine emergency. How to access the feature may vary depending on the brand you carry. On an iPhone, for example, you would press and hold the side/home button and volume up or down. Sonny pointed out that the SOS call feature is automatically modified to your destination. This feature will connect you with the equivalent of the local 911 service. No need to do anything differently. Of course, it's always better to avoid trouble first. Keep the contact information of a taxi company or a local driver in your phone. At night, when alone or unsure, err on the side of caution and get a ride.

I also suggest you map the area first, particularly upon arrival to a new city and when you will be more vulnerable, such as when carrying a bag or at night. Don't walk around with your head buried in your phone following a line on the maps app. In the bigger cities, have a general sense of where you are headed and read up about the areas you'll visit. This doesn't mean you can't enjoy casually wandering around the streets of the Trastevere district in Rome. Once you know a neighborhood is okay in larger metropolitan areas, have fun. Smaller destinations are typically low risk. Mapping in advance probably isn't necessary if you spend the afternoon roaming around Bellagio in Lake Como, at a little seaside town, or a Tuscan village, for example.

Terrorism and Disasters

As the US State Department mentions, terrorist groups have shown an interest in plotting attacks in Italy. While a relatively low risk, should attacks occur, areas of high tourist traffic may be targets. There's no harm in simply taking note of points of egress. Get on any airplane, and it won't leave the ground until this information has been reviewed. While some of these scenarios are black swan events, the few seconds you take to plan for the unexpected might save your life. Beyond that, what if there were a fire or earthquake, and you had to exit as soon as possible? Earthquakes are common in Italy, and many buildings are ancient. Would you know how to get out? What if the main door was blocked? Did you note an alternative way out? If the nightclub you were in was filled with smoke, would you be prepared with a few options for escape? There's no need to be paranoid but being aware is a smart practice in an unfamiliar setting.

Thieves as Impersonators

Some thieves are creative, and there have even been reports of impersonating police officers. Franco Spaccialbelli of the Hotel Montecarlo in Rome told me about several guests who were approached by individuals who declared they were plainclothes police conducting an inspection of counterfeit currency. You can probably guess what happened next. The victims handed over their money and never saw it again. It's improbable that a plainclothes police officer is interested in a tourist minding their own business. Use good judgment. When in doubt, ask anyone brandishing a police badge who stops you to call a uniformed officer. In the age of Covid-19, I heard from a solo female traveler that she was approached by a male dressed like the Trenitalia employees. He demanded that she leave the waiting area and come with him for a temperature check. Something didn't feel right. She resisted and questioned the individual, who became agitated and walked away. While we can't know the true motive, the lesson is if something doesn't feel right, trust your instincts. New scams often emerge so to get a pulse on a dynamic situation, visit online travel forums, including Facebook groups, which have a wealth of information and allow users to ask questions.

Traffic

Traffic can be erratic in Italy, and drivers don't always follow traffic signals or wait for pedestrians to cross. If a driver knows you see them when you're entering a crosswalk, they may cut you off. I've found that when crossing a busy street, it can be effective not to make direct eye contact with a motorist but monitor them with peripheral vision. They will be less likely to cut you off if they don't think you see them. Another reason to be cautious after dark is that I've seen cars disregard traffic signals in cities late at night as they race down city streets several times the speed limit.

Vulnerable Arrival Window

I begin preparing for arrival from the time I get situated on the airplane. I ensure my passport is in an internal upper body zipper pocket when possible. When the wheels finally touch down, chances are you will be excited, exhausted, and disorientated, particularly if you landed after a long, international flight. In the airport, hundreds of people may be around, and the context is entirely different—the language, mannerisms, dress, sights, sounds, smells, and customs. Do what you can to get a few hours of sleep on the flight. If melatonin or Tylenol PM works for you, great (just don't start a new routine on the plane and risk being groggier when you arrive). Upon arrival, it pays to be extra vigilant, especially once you get to baggage claim. It can also pay to travel light. Excessive and cumbersome baggage makes you more vulnerable.

As you leave the airport (Rome is infamous for this), you may be asked if you need a ride or airport transfer. Keep a firm hand on your luggage and ignore everyone who approaches you. Go right to the taxi stand and get in line. Alternatively, there are authorized booths in the airport that can help with transportation. Assume that anyone approaching you is not licensed, and you have no idea what they will charge you or, even worse, if they have nefarious intent. It's best if your ground transportation can bring you directly to your lodging. When first arriving, although it may cost more, I suggest you splurge to safely get where you are going, especially if you're unfamiliar with the destination. Dragging luggage from a metro or bus to your lodging makes you stand out as a visitor. Having extra baggage and being jetlagged only compounds your susceptibility. I'm a firm believer that deliberate packing is a must for travel, so in the following chapter, I'll discuss how I approach that in detail.

XII

Packing: Light is Right

Travel light. Live light. Spread the light. Be the light.
—YOGI BHAJAN

Regarding packing, I can't recall anyone ever saying they wished they had brought more stuff. On the other hand, scores of students, friends, and those I've talked to over the years have lamented about overpacking. When they return, they feel bogged down, buy extra suitcases to fit everything, or make difficult choices about leaving articles behind. Often these travelers pay overweight fees at the airport when returning home.

Traveling with excess luggage is a burden that makes you less mobile. Italy has narrow corridors and cobblestone streets, and you may need to cover long distances on them to reach your destinations. Avoid taking large suitcases, as they may not fit into places like taxi trunks and train compartments. When there are elevators, they can be tiny and slow, and you'll need to carry a bag up seemingly endless stairs when there aren't. Large, unwieldy bags don't make train travel fun and can leave you feeling vulnerable as you get from point A to point B.

Beyond that, bags have the tendency to expand. On your first time in Italy, you will accumulate things like souvenirs, gifts, new shoes, soaps and perfumes, food, coffee, candy, and clothes you didn't even know you'd fall in love with. And if you are returning, you may come back with that item you didn't manage to get last time, along with many unexpected treasures.

My philosophy is to bring a few essential items. If any unexpected needs arise, buy what you need once you're there. Nonetheless, what you should select takes careful planning. Bear in mind that these are general guidelines. If the purpose of your trip includes business, formal events, or outdoor activities such as skiing, adjust accordingly. In any case, the first thing you should do is look at the weather forecast, as there can be significant variations from north to south. I suggest you approach packing by starting with the basics. Bring enough for one week at the most since these can easily be washed, even in the bathroom sink, if necessary.

Italians typically wear long pants or jeans, even in the summer, unless at the beach. Well-fitting jeans are always in style for all genders and ages. In addition, I suggest one to two additional pairs of pants. If you prefer skirts and dresses, you can substitute them. If you know that you're heading to the beach, flip-flops, shorts, tank tops, and a swim outfit make sense. I always bring a long-sleeved shirt and an appropriately thick sweater depending on the time of year. Having at least one button-down, wrinkle-free, oxford-style shirt can be helpful for men (and I always select fabrics that wrinkle the least). Muted colors of several nondescript shirts (long or short sleeves, depending on the weather) or polos are a great addition. A jacket with some water resistance comes in handy, heavier for the winter and lighter for summer. And something comfortable to sleep in will help you relax after a long day. For colder months, a scarf is recommended. However, these can easily be purchased in Italy, are inexpensive, and can be unique.

Your choice of footwear is one of the most important. Typically, even in cities, it's common for visitors to log 20-30,000 steps each day. Your travels could take you to hiking trails, uneven cobblestone streets, and up many stairs. High heels are best left at home. There's nothing wrong with a stylish, clean pair of athletic shoes. I always bring a pair of running sneakers with comfortable inserts for exercise and when my feet need extra support. In addition, I choose one other pair of shoes, ideally, something that is stylish yet comfortable and roadworthy. Brands like Merrell and Geox are two of my favorites.

Remember that you can wash just about everything by hand in a sink, at a laundromat, or potentially at your hotel. If you book an Airbnb, check if it has a washer. If you need something, use the opportunity to have fun exploring one of the local markets and buy some inexpensive new clothes or, depending on your budget, spend a bit more at a department store or boutique. When I pack, I lay it all out on a bed, look it over, and usually remove a few items, keeping what is necessary.

In addition to the above items, here are some items you shouldn't leave without:

- Prescription medications and documentation of the prescription. If it is something critical, bring a week's supply extra and split it up in your bags. Should something get lost, or you end up delayed in Italy, this will buy you time to figure out how to refill.
- High-quality ziplock bags are challenging to find in Italy and useful when traveling. I use them to pack my liquid toiletries (hint: get travel sizes) and bring a few extra for items that could leak.
- Sunscreen is available in Italy, but I prefer small travel tubes that easily fit in a bag or pocket.
- Tissues are good to have in case of poorly stocked restrooms, and using hand sanitizer may help keep you healthy when you can't wash your hands.
- A medicine kit should be on your list. Include a travel-size container of Advil or Tylenol, bandages, antibiotic cream, Benadryl, anti-diarrhea pills, cold or flu tablets, antacids, eyedrops, or items you find you occasionally need. You can get equivalents in Italy, but if you are delayed during travel, become ill on the airplane or at an inconvenient time, these

provide a safety net. Think carefully about anyone else you are responsible for. For example, what will you do if you are traveling with children and one spikes a fever on the plane? In this case, bring a thermometer and the medicines you prefer.

- An eye mask and earplugs may help block overhead lighting and noisy neighbors on your flights, so you get to sleep.

- Remember all necessary electronics and their chargers. Headphones may be convenient should you have time to kill while traveling. You will also want to ensure your phone is backed up to the cloud. If it gets lost or stolen, you also don't want to lose your data.

- A small well-constructed bag is nice to secure items as you travel around town, especially for things that are too bulky for pockets; a crossbody bag (even a fanny pack) you can position in front of your chest or waist does the job. A small bag or backpack for day trips, which could be your carry-on, is convenient. Lastly, a compressible reusable grocery bag will come in handy as grocery stores charge for bags, which tend to be weak and not the best to handle heavy items.

With this list, you may be able to fit everything into a carry-on bag and a personal bag. This is my preference. Luggage gets lost, sometimes returned in a few hours, days, or never. Regardless, your personal carry-on bag should contain everything you can't function without. This is distinct from your larger carry-on. It should be small enough that it won't be gate-checked on a regional connecting flight and could be stowed under your seat if necessary, but large enough to include essential documents, a medicine kit, prescription medicines (and documentation), electronics, underwear, socks, and an extra shirt. If your bag is misplaced, you'll be happy to have something to change into. I suggest your passport, wallet, and critical prescriptions stay on your person.

Here is a suggested packing list, in addition to the clothes you'll wear on your travel to Italy:

Clothes

Underwear and socks, 5-7
Pants, dresses, or skirts, 2-3
Shirts, 3-4 (long or short sleeves and weight, depending on
 time of travel)
Button down, dressier shirt or blouse, 1-2
Sweater, 1-2 (weight depending on time of travel)
Comfortable shoes, 2 pairs, and insoles for shoes
Water resistant jacket (weight depending on time of travel)
Swim or beach attire, if applicable
Hat, scarf, gloves (winter)

Additional items

ELECTRONICS

Phone charger
Electrical adapter
Headphones

DURING TRAVEL

Medicine kit
Prescription medications, including extra, and a copy of
 prescription
Travel-sized sunscreen
Travel-sized toiletries
Travel-sized tissues
Hand sanitizer

Eye mask & earplugs
Travel laundry detergent
Several ziplock bags

BAGS

Cloth or reusable shopping bag
Backpack or day trip bag
Small crossbody bag

Thoughts on Planning Return Travel

I always recommend staying in the city of your international flight the night before your departure. I don't want to chance taking a train, bus, or even connecting flight to get to the Italian city of my departure. Flights later in the day can also be problematic as lines get longer, and problems on earlier flights accumulate later. Furthermore, I feel it's helpful to go direct to your home country from Italy. If you must make a connection, do it on your home turf. You won't be stranded in a foreign country if something goes wrong or you miss the connection.

XIII

Keeping the Magic Alive

One's destination is never a place, but a new way of seeing things.
—HENRY MILLER

If you've ever had a genuinely relaxing or inspiring trip, you will notice that your entire mindset is different. Travel seems to be good for the spirit. Once you get home and unpack your bag, it can feel like you've still got some magic dust left, leaving you suspended between two versions of reality, perhaps for a few days. Once your jet lag passes, this magic doesn't have to leave you. Instead, it can be an opportunity to be proactive about those fleeting moments of inspiration, or to have thoughts about living differently. This isn't to say you must assume another identity and "become Italian." Instead, it's the appreciation you've gained through your experiences and finding ways to tap into what left you inspired, relaxed, or intellectually engaged.

Italy offers one the most priceless of one's possessions
—one's own soul.
—BARBARA GRIZZUTI HARRISON

In my case, Roman history gave me the teachings of Marcus Aurelius, which undoubtedly helped me navigate some difficult times in my life. The artistic heritage I observed in Italy motivated me to rediscover a childhood love of drawing and painting. Trying new foods, where attention was given to quality, drove me to fine-tune my cooking skills. Cherished moments with family and the reminder of the sacred mealtime ritual reawakened a weekly tradition. Many Sundays, we cook a homemade meal to share together. I became so enamored with Italian espresso I took a barista course in Florence. I don't start a morning without making a cappuccino. Ultimately, what you do will be incorporated into a new identity. What did you find yourself appreciating during your travels? Italian creativity, looking at life from a fresh perspective, learning about history, taking evening walks? Pick something and make it a habit. It will bring you new opportunities you never imagined. Habit expert James Clear says that identity is the key to behavior change. For example, you can think *I am a cultured person who appreciates art. I reminded myself about this in Italy. I will seek out local expositions and incorporate more of the arts into my life each month.*

The Italian language also became part of my life in a very personal way. Being of Italian origins, I knew that when my son, Alessandro, was born, there was no question he would have an Italian name. I also wanted to give him something I never got—a second language. Although my grandparents grew up in Italy, coming from regions with different dialects, they mostly communicated in English. My grandmother's heavily accented speech was colored with some choice phrases in her Neapolitan dialect. Even as a young boy, I knew not to repeat them.

I got my first real taste of Italian when I was twelve years old. Yes, this was that trip where I ate my aunt's dog food. My family had traveled with my grandfather to the mountainous village of his youth near L'Aquila. I loved everything about it. The crowing of roosters was my alarm clock. I also ate rabbit for the first (and last) time, started lifelong friendships with my *abruzzesi* cousins, and reveled in the challenge of communicating. I had no choice but to learn Italian, embarking on a journey that began with memorizing Italian on cassette tapes. I returned to Italy to earn a master's degree in Milan, and later again for work. As a non-native speaker, I may never be completely satisfied with my Italian fluency. But that wasn't going to get in the way of teaching Alessandro.

Since I first held him, I have exclusively spoken to my son in

Italian. I sang and played Italian folk songs I learned in Abruzzo. As a baby, "*Campagnola Bella*" was the only one that soothed his crying. I found there were some words I had never learned, like diaper, gears, drain, puddle, playground equipment, rubber ducky, and construction vehicles. I looked them up and watched YouTube videos to check pronunciation. I invested in a multi-region DVD player and have amassed an impressive collection of Italian language materials: scores of DVDs featuring Alessandro's favorite cartoons and children's books; *Il piccolissimo Bruco Maisazio* and *Prosciutto e Uova Verdi* are two we've especially come to love. When Alessandro picks an English book, I translate it into Italian as best I can. Most Sundays, we learn about Italy together as we watch Rai Italia's *Linea Verde* over a cappuccino and Mulino Bianco cookies.

As he began forming words, Alessandro said *sì* before yes and *bottiglia* (bottle) was one of the first things out of his mouth. At preschool, he would tell the teacher he needed to wash his *mani* (hands) and discuss the Coniglio di Pasqua (Easter Bunny). He is English-dominant but understands me completely and even gets annoyed if I try to speak to him in English. One day, when he was four years old, I said, "*Oggi facciamo tiramisu*." He gave me a bewildered look and replied, "You're too heavy!" We had never made tiramisu before, yet he understood that the dessert literally translated to "pick me up." I was beaming with pride. In that moment, I realized that my son, born to American parents, would forever be connected to his roots.

Your journey to Italy can be more than a vacation. It can be a rich cultural experience. It can become part of who you are. By now, you have the context, basic knowledge of customs and the culture, and an understating of the language to approach Italy. This book cannot teach you everything, but I'm hopeful it will get you started down a path that will take you on one of the most enriching trips of your life.

> *Do not follow where the path may lead, go instead*
> *where there is no path and leave a trail.*
> —RALPH WALDO EMERSON

Appendix

Essentials

Sì	Yes
No	No
Mi chiamo...	My name is...
Per favore	please
Grazie	thank you
Piacere	nice to meet you
buongiorno	good morning; good day
buonasera	good (late) afternoon; evening
la mattina	morning
il pomeriggio	afternoon
la sera	evening
ieri	yesterday
oggi	today
domani	tomorrow
scusi	excuse me
Permesso?	May I get through or come in?
aiuto	Help
Mi dispiace	I'm sorry.
Non capisco	I don't understand.
Come si dice...?	How do you say...?
Non parlo italiano.	I don't speak Italian.
Parla inglese?	Do you speak English?
prego	You're welcome; go ahead
Dov'è il bagno?	Where is the bathroom?
libero	free; available

occupato . . . . occupied
gratis; gratuito . . . . free of charge
C'è. . . . . Is there...?; There is...
Ci sono... . . . . Are there?; There are...
Perché? . . . . Why?
Che cosa? . . . . What?
Chi?. . . . . Who?
Come? . . . . How?
Quando? . . . . When?
Dove?. . . . . Where?
Quale? . . . . Which?

Numbers

uno . . . . one
due . . . . two
tre . . . . three
quattro . . . . four
cinque . . . . five
sei. . . . . six
sette . . . . seven
otto . . . . eight
nove. . . . . nine
dieci . . . . ten
undici . . . . eleven
dodici. . . . . twelve
tredici . . . . thirteen
quattrodici. . . . . fourteen
quindici . . . . fifteen
sedici. . . . . sixteen
diciassete . . . . seventeen
diciotto . . . . eighteen
diciannove. . . . . nineteen
venti . . . . twenty
trenta . . . . thirty
quaranta . . . . forty

cinquanta . . . . fifty

sessanta . . . . sixty

settanta. . . . . seventy

ottanta . . . . eighty

novanta . . . . ninety

cento . . . . one hundred

mille . . . . one thousand

cinquemila . . . . five thousand

un milione . . . . one million

Days and Time

lunedì . . . . Monday

martedì . . . . Tuesday

mercoledì. . . . . Wednesday

giovedì. . . . . Thursday

venerdì . . . . Friday

sabato . . . . Saturday

domenica . . . . Sunday

un minuto . . . . a minute

un'ora . . . . an hour

un giorno . . . . a day

una settimana . . . . a week

un mese. . . . . a month

un anno . . . . a year

Months

gennaio . . . . January

febbraio . . . . February

marzo . . . . March

aprile . . . . April

maggio . . . . May

giugno . . . . June

luglio . . . . July

agosto . . . . August

settembre . . . . September

ottobre . . . . October
novembre . . . . November
dicembre . . . . December

Eating Out

Sono da solo/a. (masc./fem.). . . . . I'm by myself.
Siamo in (due, tre, quarto). . . . . There are (2,3, 4...) of us.
Il menu, per favore. . . . . The menu, please.
il cameriere/la cameriera (masc./fem.) . . the server
Il conto, per favore. . . . . The check, please.
Sono pronto/a. (masc./fem.) . . . . I'm ready.
È buono/a. . . . . It is good.
Mi piace/piacciono. . . . . I like (singular noun)/(plural noun)
Ho sete. . . . . I'm thirsty.
Per me. . . . . I'll have...
Non mi va, grazie. . . . . I can't eat any more, thank you.
Potrei averne un altro po', per favore? . . . Could I have some more, please?
ancora. . . . . more
(Non) Ho fame. I'm (not) hungry.
(Non) Mangio. . . . . I (don't) eat...
(Non) Bevo. . . . . I (don't) drink...
un tavolo . . . . a table
antipasto. . . . . starter
il primo . . . . first course
il secondo . . . . second course
il contorno . . . . side dish, vegetables
l'insalata . . . . salad
la frutta fresca . . . . fresh fruit
il dolce. . . . . dessert
il coltello . . . . knife
la forchetta . . . . fork
il cucchiaio . . . . spoon
vino della casa . . . . house wine
acqua naturale/gassata . . . . flat/sparkling water
una bottiglia . . . . a bottle

Sono allergico/a. (masc./fem.) . . . . I'm allergic.
le noci . . . . walnuts (generic word for nuts)
le noccioline. peanuts
i latticini . . . . dairy products
il lattosio . . . . lactose
il glutine . . . . gluten
il pesce . . . . fish
le uova. . . . . eggs
le verdure. . . . . vegetables
la carne . . . . meat
Sono vegetariano/a. (masc./fem.) . . . . . . I'm a vegetarian.
la mancia . . . . the tip
Cosa mi consiglia? . . . . What do you suggest?
Buon appetito!. . . . . Enjoy!
Salute! . . . . Cheers!
il piatto del giorno . . . . the daily special
da portare via . . . . for takeaway
Potrei assaggiare? . . . . Could I taste?/Could I try some?
Posso provare? . . . . Can I try this on?
caldo . . . . hot
freddo . . . . cold

Shopping

Mi dica./Dimmi. . . . . How can I help you?
Do un'occhiata. . . . . I'm browsing.
Non ho ancora deciso. . . . . I haven't decided yet.
Avete...? . . . . Do you have?
Ho bisogno di... . . . . I need...
Posso? . . . . May I?
questo . . . . this
quello. . . . . that
più piccolo. . . . . smaller
più grande. . . . . bigger
un pezzo . . . . A piece
un po' . . . . a little

quattro, cinque...fette . . . . four, five...slices

due, tre...etti . . . . two, three...hundred grams

bancomat. . . . . ATM or debit card

la carta (di credito) . . . . credit card

in contanti . . . . cash

costoso . . . . expensive

economico . . . . affordable

uno sconto . . . . a discount

saldi . . . . sales

la taglia . . . . the size (clothes)

il numero . . . . the size (shoes)

È bello. . . . . It's nice.

locale. . . . . local

aperto . . . . open

chiuso . . . . closed

Travel

Vorrei un biglietto per... . . . . I'd like a ticket for...

Vorrei partire/ritornare. . . . . I'd like to depart/arrive...

partenza . . . . departure

Arrivo. . . . . arrival

Quanto costa? . . . . How much does it cost?

Quando parte? . . . . When does it depart?

Da quale binario parte? . . . . Which platform does it leave
from?

È questo il treno per...? . . . . Is this the train that goes to...

Quando arriva? . . . . When does it arrive?

solo andata . . . . one way

andata e ritorno . . . . round trip

Scendo. . . . . I'm getting off.

entrata . . . . entrance

uscita . . . . exit

la fermata . . . . the stop

il biglietto . . . . ticket

il binario . . . . platform/track

cambiare treno . . . . change trains
il controllo . . . . ticket check
fare il biglietto . . . . buy a ticket
l'orario . . . . schedule
il posto . . . . seat
prenotato . . . . reserved
lo sportello . . . . ticket window
la stazione. . . . . the station
in arrivo . . . . arriving
il viaggiatore . . . . traveler
lo sciopero . . . . the strike
prima seconda/classe . . . . first/second class
convalidare/timbrare . . . . validate
la valiga. . . . . bag
in arrivo/partenza . . . . arriving/leaving
in ritardo . . . . late
l'autobus . . . . the bus
la metro. . . . . the metro
un battello (un traghetto) . . . . ferry
un aliscafo . . . . high speed ferry
un tram . . . . a streetcar

Directions

Dov'è...? . . . . Where is...?
Giri... . . . . Turn
destra . . . . right
sinistra . . . . left
l'incrocio . . . . the intersection
il semaforo. . . . . the traffic light
dopo . . . . after
prima. . . . . before
in fondo . . . . at the end
diritto . . . . straight
la piazza . . . . the town square

Emergencies

Sto male.	I am sick.
Ho bisogno di un dottore.	I need a doctor.
la farmacia	the pharmacy
la ricetta	the prescription
l'ospedale	the hospital
il pronto soccorso.	the emergency room
la medicina	medicine
Chiami la polizia.	Call the police
Chiami un ambulanza.	Call an ambulance.
Aiuto!	Help!
Lasciami stare!	Leave me alone!

Glossary

l'abbigliamento, a general term for clothing shop

gli agnolotti, a small meat-filled pasta

un agriturismo, a small farm that offers food and rooms for visitors

un albergo, hotel

un alimentari, small neighborhood grocery store

un aliscafo, high speed ferry boat

americanata, a pejorative meaning excessively American in style

andare, to go

un antipasto, appetizer (might include sliced meats, toasts, cheeses, pâtés)

un aperitivo, the custom of a pre-meal drink accompanied by snacks

un architetto, architect

l'autostrada, Italy's toll highway

avere, to have

il bagno, the bathroom

il bancomat, ATM machine or refers to a debit card

il bar di fiducia, one's regular coffee bar

un bar, an Italian café that serves espresso

il barbiere, a barber shop

un battello or un traghetto, ferry

il bel paese, the beautiful country

negozio di biancheria, a store that specializes in undergarments and linens

un bicchiere d'acqua, a glass of water

il binario, train platform

il bollito, a stew of boiled meats and vegetables

le botteghe, smaller specialized shops

la bresaola, cured beef

una brioche or un cornetto, croissant

una brutta figura, poor impression

Buon Anno, Happy New Year

buon appetito, enjoy your meal

buon pomeriggio, good afternoon

buona giornata, have a nice day

buona serata, have a nice evening

buonasera, good evening

buongiorno, good morning or good day

un caffè americano, an espresso with hot water added

un caffè macchiato, an espresso with a few drops of steamed milk on top

un caffè, a coffee (usually espresso)

il capitone, a female eel

un cappuccino, an espresso with four ounces (125 ml) of steamed milk and froth

la cartoleria, a stationery store that could also sell books, gifts, etc.

il casatiello, festival bread, filled with ingredients such as hard-boiled eggs, pancetta, salame, provolone, etc.

la cena, dinner

le ciabatte, house slippers

ciao, hi (informal)

il citofono, intercom

la colazione, breakfast

la Colomba, a dove-shaped cake popular during Easter

il coperto, service charge for bread and sitting down

il corso, avenue

i crotti, caves in Chiavenna area used to store food

dare, to give

Denominazione di Origine Controllata (DOC), Designation of Controlled Origin is a very highly controlled wine with specific rules on the origin of the grapes and the production methods

Denominazione di Origine Controllata e Garantita (DOCG), Designation of Controlled Origin Guaranteed is the strictest designation for Italian wines with a "guarantee" that they are the highest quality

Denominazione d'Origine Protetta (DOP), Protected Designation of Origin food product

dottore (masculine) or *dottoressa (feminine),* physician or a title for anyone with a university degree *dovere,* to have to

l'edicola, the newstand

eletrodomestici, an electronics store

entrata libera, free entrance to a shop (meaning browsing encouraged)

essere, to be

etti, 100-gram units

fare una bella figura, make a good impression

fare, to do or to make

farmacia di turno, pharmacy on duty

una farmacia, a pharmacy

feriale, working days (typically all days of the year except Sundays and holidays)

Ferragosto, the holiday period in August when most Italians take vacations

ferramenta, a hardware store

festivo, public holiday or feast day.

flâneur, French term that refers to an urban explorer

il formaggio, the cheese

il/la fornaio/a, the baker

il forno, la panetteria, il panettiere, or il fornaio, a bakery with assorted breads, cookies, sweets, and pizzas

la freccia, the bullet train

la frutta, the fruit

fruttivendolo or negozio di frutta e verdura, a fruit and vegetable store or stand

gentile, kind

Imposta sul Valore Aggiunto (IVA), value-added tax (VAT)

Indicazione Geografica Protetta (IGP), Protected Geographical Indication food product

Indicazione Geografica Tipica (IGT), is representative of a wine typical of the geographical region

l'infermiera, the nurse

l'ingegnere, the engineer

l'Intercity, intercity train

un latte macchiato, like a cappuccino but with more milk and less froth

la lavanderia, the laundromat

la libreria, the bookstore

locale or nostrano, produced locally

la macelleria, the butcher shop

un marocchino, a mini mocha or mini cappuccino with the addition of chocolate

il mercato, the market or food market

la mesticheria, a store that sells items for the home and some hardware

la moquette, wall-to-wall carpeting

Natale, Christmas

la nave, the ship

il negozio, the store

non toccare, do not touch

la nonna, the grandma

l'ostello, the youth hostel

l'osteria, interchangeable with trattoria but may focus more on drinks than food

le Pagine Gialle, the Yellow Pages

il pane carasau, a crispy flatbread from Sardinia

la paninoteca, a shop specializing in sandwiches

la parrucchieria, a hair salon that serves women and sometimes men

Pasqua, Easter

Pasquetta, an Italian holiday the Monday after Easter

la passeggiata, the Italian cultural practice of strolling

la pasticceria, a fancier sweets shop with cakes and the kind of small artisan pastries

la pastiera napoletana, a creamy cake made with ricotta, eggs, dough, cooked grain, citrus, and other ingredients

la pensione, a low-budget hotel

i peperoni, peppers

per favore, per piacere, or per cortesia, please

la profumeria, a shop selling soaps and perfumes

la pizza alla diavola, pizza with spicy pepperoni (cured meat)

i pizzoccheri, buckwheat pasta of Valtellina

il ponte, literally bridge (refers to when a midweek holiday is extended (or is bridged) through the weekend

la porta, the door or city gate

potere, to be able to

il pranzo, the lunch

il primo, the first course (usually pasta, rice dishes, polenta, or soup)

una produzione propria, made in house

un regionale, a regional train

il Ricaricard, a card for adding credit to phones

un ristorante, a more formal restaurant but may also refer to eateries in general

la salumeria, a delicatessen that specializes in cooked, cured, or smoked meats, commonly made of pork, and some cheeses

scolastico, when schools are in session

il secondo, second course (usually meat or fish)

servizio al tavolo, table service

lo sfilatino, Italian baguette

la signora, miss or madam

il signore, mister or sir

il soffritto, sautéed herbs, carrots, onions, and celery

gli spaghetti alle vongole, spaghetti with clams

stabilimenti, bagni, or lido, beach clubs

stare, to be (use for discussing wellness)

gli struffoli, a dessert made of small balls of dough in syrup

surgelato, frozen

il supermercato, the supermarket

la tabaccheria, shop that sells tobacco and many odds and ends

una tavola calda or una rosticceria, prepared foods shop

una torrefazione, coffee roaster

una trattoria, a family-operated restaurant that serves in a home-cooked style

uscire, to go out

una villa, a stand-alone house

vino della casa, house wine

volere, to want

Common Holidays

Patron saint festival *(Festa del santo patrono)*
Dates vary across towns and cities

New Year's Day *(Capodanno)*
1 January

Epiphany *(Epifania)*
6 January

Easter Sunday *(Pasqua)*
Varies annually

Easter Monday *(Pasquetta)*
Monday after Easter

Liberation Day *(Festa della Liberazione)*
25 April

Labor Day *(Festa del Lavoro)*
1 May

Republic Day *(Festa della Repubblica)*
2 June

Assumption Day *(Assunzione/Ferragosto)*
15 August

All Saints' Day *(Ognissanti)*
1 November

Immaculate Conception (*Immacolata Concezione*)
8 December

Christmas Day (*Natale*)
25 December

Saint Stephen's Day (*Santo Stefano*)
26 December

New Year's Eve (*San Silvestro*)
31 December
*not an official holiday, although many Italians have a big dinner lasting until midnight

Printed in Great Britain
by Amazon